The Rise & Fall of Nottingham's Railway Network

Volume 1

Lines in the City

Hayden J Reed

With thanks to my parents for putting up with the trains when I lived at home

Contents

Introduction

Nottingham, like many other cities in the Midlands embraced the railway age. By the start of the Twentieth Century, four national companies had built infrastructure in the City, with some 21 passenger stations serving the immediate City area alone. Economic trends, shifting modes of transport and politics have progressively eroded this network and a century on, little of it remains.

A number of books have been published about Nottingham's railways over the years, and its early history is well documented. It can be argued that these works fall into two categories. These are photograph albums with limited historical background; or detailed academic works with a wealth of information. Both formats are worthy and offer much to the casual reader. This work attempts to combine the two styles however, offering a wealth of photographs and plans, supported by technical and historical background. It also considers the decline of the system, and the subsequent destruction of much of our Victorian engineering heritage, something seldom covered in other works.

The Author grew up in Nottingham in the Sixties and Seventies, when derelict rail routes still criss-crossed the City and its suburbs. Fascinated by disused structures and abandoned track beds, he began photographing them from his early teens. The interest has followed him through two decades of working as a Civil Engineer for Nottingham's Highway Authority.

In the course of his career the Author has gained access to many places inaccessible to the general public. This has enabled him to record images of numerous Victorian railway structures that have since been demolished or buried and forgotten. The resulting archive, supported with previously unpublished photographs of the network in its heyday, historic material, plans and diagrams has been brought together to create a unique record of the rise, decline and ultimate fall of Nottingham's railway network.

Volume One broadly covers the main conurbation of Nottingham as it was at the start of the Twentieth Century (within the marked box on the map opposite). It considers the three principal stations that the City once boasted, the urban and suburban commuter lines and the busy locomotive sheds of Nottingham and Colwick.

The second volume covers the outer reaches of the City, up to a radius of about 10 miles, and includes the coalfield lines to the north, and cross country lines to the east.

Many of the photographs in this work are the Authors own work, but where other Photographers material has been kindly loaned, this has been credited as appropriate. All network maps and diagrams are copyrighted to the Author unless stated otherwise.

H J Reed, March 2007

Above : London Road High Level Station was just one of many to close in the Nottingham area in the Sixties. Like several others, it found a fresh use after the railway had gone. It lingered on until 2006, when it was demolished to make way for new development. Today demand for development land has meant that very few abandoned railway sites now remain.

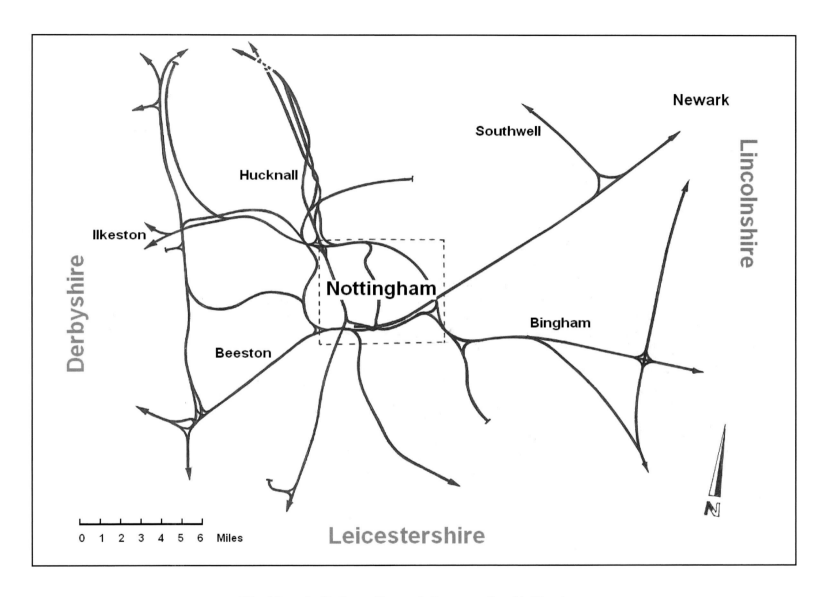

The Historic Railway Network Surrounding Nottingham

Nottingham once sat at the hub of a substantial railway network, as the plan above shows. Much of it was built during the latter part of the Nineteenth century when "Railwaymania" gripped the country, and rival companies were scrambling to reach the same markets. In the Twenty first Century, very little of this labyrinth now exists. Volume One explores the rise and fall of the railways within "metropolitan" Nottingham, shown in the central box. Volume Two takes a look at the wider picture, and those lines that ran beyond the immediate City limits.

1. The Midland Railway in Nottingham
Lenton South Junction to Sneinton Junction

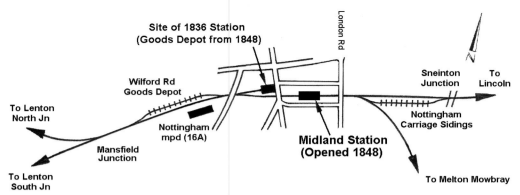

The Midland Railway in Nottingham Circa 1900

The plan above shows the principal lines and facilities on the Midland Railway in Nottingham at the start of the Twentieth Century. A third Midland Station was built in 1904 on the site of the second (1848) station to compete with the GCR.

South Elevation of the Porte Cochere and clock tower of A E Lambert's 1904 Art-nouveau station. This was the third Midland Station to be built in Nottingham.

Nottm City Council / BDP / Gleeds

Three Midland Stations

The present Nottingham Station is not the first, or even the second to occupy the area around Carrington Street. The original Midland Counties Railway Station was opened in 1839, and sited to the west side of Carrington Street, virtually opposite the end of Station Street. It was a west facing terminus, with two platforms flanking a train shed and a range of two storey classically styled stone buildings to the front.

In 1846 the newly formed Midland Railway pushed east from Nottingham to Lincoln. As services developed the station became increasingly unsatisfactory and cramped. In 1848 the Midland took the decision to rebuild the station to the east of Carrington Street level crossing, with a new entrance on Station Street. The old station became used as a goods depot.

The new facilities allowed for through running and were capable of handling far greater numbers of trains than its predecessor. The main station buildings were constructed in a combination of local red brick and limestone. The architecture was relatively plain, but exhibited classical influences, with a row of stone columns facing a portico to the front. On the platforms, passengers were sheltered from the elements by glazed canopies which extended for half of their length.

Some 20 years on from the opening of this second station, similar problems to those experienced with the first began to emerge. The local network had developed, and passenger throughput had increased as a consequence. The cramped goods facilities at the old station restricted growth in freight traffic, and the level crossing on Carrington Street had become a major inconvenience to road users and railway operation. The Midland was also facing increasing pressure from its arch rival, the Great Northern Railway, who had acquired the nearby London Road Station, through amalgamation with the provincial Ambergate, Boston, Nottingham & Eastern Junction Railway in 1862, and who offered a competing service to London, via Grantham.

The solution found by the Midland Railway was to buy the West Croft canal, which ran parallel to, and south of the railway, together with additional land fronting Queens Road. The canal was filled in, an extra platform built, and the station facilities given a face-lift. To the south, goods avoiding lines and sidings were laid out to ease the congestion problem. The road traffic problem on Carrington Street was also resolved, much to the relief of the Nottingham Corporation, through construction of a multiple span wrought iron bridge, which still stands today.

This second station would probably still exist, had it not been for the arrival of another rival company in 1899. The Great Central Railway was a relative latecomer, but that did not stop it occupying a prime site in the centre of the city. The magnificent new station that it built in partnership with the Great Northern was arguably the finest in the East Midlands. Christened Nottingham Victoria in 1900, its elegant Renaissance frontage and landmark clock tower led through to three cavernous train sheds and twelve platforms. Travelling south, expresses bound for Marylebone strode across the Midland tracks to at the western end of its station on an enormous bowstring steel bridge. The whole enterprise left the Midland literally and figuratively in the shade.

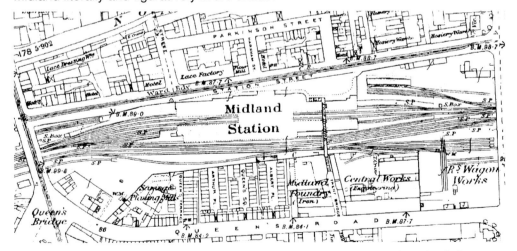

The second Midland Station is seen above in its final form on this extract from the Ordnance Survey of around 1901. The West Croft Canal ran along the line of the southernmost tracks, before turning north at the western end of the station, to pass beneath Station Street. It was filled in during 1868 to accommodate expansion of the station. Prior to 1875, a small locomotive roundhouse was situated in the corner between Station Street and London Road. This was replaced by a much larger facility on Wilford Road.

Meeting the Great Central's Challenge

The Midland's response to the Great Central's challenge was to embark on the design and construction of a new station to rival Victoria. It recruited A E Lambert, the Architect that had designed Victoria Station to work on the new project.

Midland Compound No 40935 sits in Platform 3 with the RCTS Lincolnshire Railtour in 1954. These compact engines were responsible for many passenger workings in the area, from their introduction in 1920, until final withdrawal in the late Fifties. This example spent many years based at Nottingham Shed.

C A Hill

The existing road bridge on Carrington Street was widened, and in 1903 a handsome new station building in a distinctive Art Nouveau style started to rise up. Faced in terracotta, it comprised a 200 foot long Porte Cochere, with an elegant baroque clock tower in the centre. Carriages would drop the wealthier passengers off here, and they would then pass through one of three doorways into the main booking hall. The large Booking Hall was ornately finished with sumptuous mouldings and a barrel vaulted roof, which incorporated a considerable glazed area, to give the space a light and airy feel.

Beyond the booking hall, passengers entered a distribution bridge, with flights of stairs connecting to three island platforms, and luggage lifts built into distinctive brick towers with pyramidal roofs, for the conveyance of trolleys to platform level.

The northerly island incorporated a bay at its eastern end, for services to Southwell. This and the central platform were provided with a range of elegant red brick buildings, incorporating waiting and refreshment rooms, toilets, offices and two small signal boxes to control shunting and pilot engine movements. Both platforms had glazed awnings covering much of their length, and two further footbridges spanned the station. The west footbridge was purely for passenger movement within the station, whilst the east footbridge extended to Station Street and Queens Road. Prospective passengers could enter from here, via ticket gates at the head of the steps to the platform. A fourth bridge to the east was not for public use, and its lifts allowed luggage trolleys to change platforms without having the go to the distribution bridge, and to access the parcels office on Station Street. The south platform only embarked passengers on one face, the rear backing on to the freight lines.

Two large signal cabins controlled primary movements. One was located to the west of Carrington Street, whilst the other sat close to the end of the bay platform (Platform 2) at the eastern end of the station.

Class 2P No 40458 sits in the centre road awaiting a pilot turn, whilst "Tilbury Tank" 41943 of Mansfield Shed stands in platform 4 with a Worksop train. When this view was recorded in the summer of 1954, little had outwardly changed since LMS days, other than the livery of the engines. The GCR bridge carrying lines to Victoria can be seen above.

C A Hill

From Edwardian Optimism to Nationalisation

Traffic had probably reached its peak by the time the station opened in 1904, with the local network having achieved maturity. The quality of the new station doubtless did much to reclaim patronage, but the nature of the route it served meant that it never quite had the glamour of Victoria, or the bustle of nearby Derby.

The local network of lines with their attendant suburban services ensured that Midland Station was a moderately busy place, but as the Twentieth Century progressed, competition from electric trams, and later motor buses and trolleybuses saw passenger figures in decline. The years of austerity and disruption that resulted from the Great War and State control of the railways did little to help, and by the early 1920s the infrastructure and services were starting to appear threadbare, compared with the optimism of the early Edwardian era. The grouping and amalgamation of the Midland Railway into the LMS was intended to reverse the situation, but the advent of the General Strike, coal shortages and the economic depression meant that little capital was available for modernisation and improvement to facilities and services.

In the days before widespread car ownership and good long distance roads, organised rail excursions to the coast were commonplace. Trains would be chartered by a variety of bodies, including workers groups, local committees and voluntary organisations, Typical destinations were the East Coast resorts, or in the case of this example, the North Wales coast.

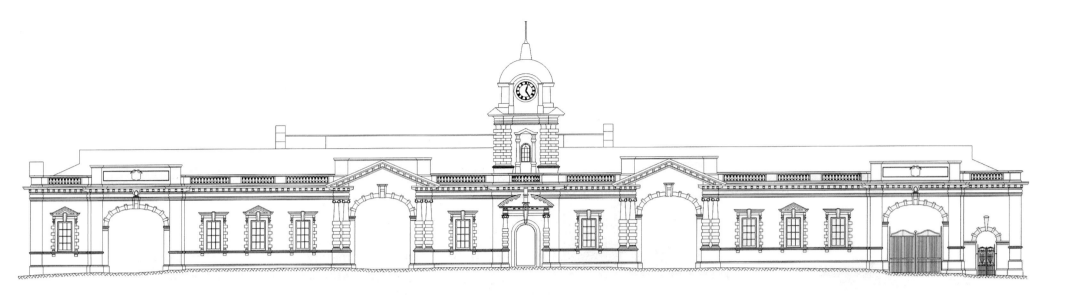

The plan above reveals the graceful design of Lambert's 1904 Midland Station. Faced in terracotta and topped with a central Baroque style clock tower, the elegance of the front elevation is perhaps less apparent on site, owing to its position on a bridge, and the difficulty of the observer to stand far enough back to see the whole frontage as a single view.

Nottm City Council / BDP / Gleeds

Ex Midland Railway Class 2P No 40454 is seen at Midland Station in about 1950. Sadly the Photographers details are not known. This locomotive was allocated to Nottingham Shed for a number of years along with several classmates.

Author's Collection

Moderate improvements were made, and the LMS made substantial investment, renewing Wilford Road bridge, and a number of other structures further out of the City. New locomotive types introduced by William Stanier, and an improving economic situation saw a gradual improvement in services through the late Thirties. By 1939 some surprisingly forward thinking had resulted in experimental diesel units operating between Nottingham and Leicester, and a shift towards operation of large capacity freight wagons, in place of traditional small vehicles.

The Second World War again set the railway system back, with any improvement programmes being set aside, and the Government taking control once more. Aside from disrupted timetables, the immediate change noticeable to the traveller was the removal of glazing from the platform canopies, as a safety precaution in case of air raids.

Air attack came in March 1941, when the carriage sidings to the east were bombed, and many coaches destroyed by fire. The neighbouring Great Northern and LNWR yards were also hit. Midland station itself escaped damage, and survived the war relatively unscathed.

In the 1950s, traffic remained reasonably buoyant, and the freight depot at Wilford Road continued to be busy. Competition from road traffic gradually took its toll however.

Freight traffic fell into sharp decline through the Sixties and by the 1970s, the extensive goods yards to the west of the station, beneath the Castle Rock lay empty. By the 1980s much of the old warehousing and sidings had gone. A large portion of railway land was redeveloped for new Inland Revenue Offices, and mixed use development, and warehousing between Wilford Road and Carrington Street, on the original 1836 station site was demolished in the early Nineties to make way for a new Magistrates Court.

Nottingham Shed (16A) was sited opposite Wilford Road Goods Yard, off Middle Furlong Road. Built in 1875, it replaced earlier facilities at the eastern end of Station Street and was home to a variety of mixed traffic, passenger and intermediate freight locomotive types. Heavy freight engine provision in the district was largely dominated by Toton in the west, and Colwick in the east.

Rebuilt Royal Scot No 46158 "The Loyal Regiment" waits for a clear road to depart east with a football special bound for London in 1959. Who Forest was playing on this occasion (and whether they won) is not known.

C A Hill

General Strikes and global conflict were not the only forms of strife to affect Midland Station. The railway had suffered occasional instances of flooding since its construction, owing to the low lying flood plain that its route follows (indeed London Road was once named Flood Road). In March 1947 however, services were badly disrupted by the worst flooding in the City's history. The situation was made worse by lack of maintenance during the war years. A flood defence scheme on the Victoria Embankment alleviated future flooding risk, but the newly created British Railways would face an uphill struggle to turn around the wider economic situation in the years following its creation at the start of 1948.

The British Railways Era

Initial investment in the newly nationalised railway, and the emergence of new classes of modern locomotives and rolling stock helped to improve the situation. As Nottingham emerged from the shadow of the war and rationing was gradually discontinued, services and conditions began to improve. Patronage remained stable, and the platforms were still crowded on summer Bank Holiday weekends. Sadly the situation was not to last.

Above : Elevation of the Cabman's shelter, situated at the south end of the Porte Cochere. This small timber building harks back to the days when handsome cabs carried wealthy patrons to and from the station. Used as a general office and store building since before the Second World War, it is destined to be restored as part of the development of the station facilities.

Nottm City Council / BDP

As the local network was closed down, and traffic declined, so did the shed's allocation. It finally closed in 1966, not quite lasting to the end of steam. It was demolished piecemeal over the next decade. A new road was built across the site in 1974 and aside from a few broken pieces of red brick wall hidden in undergrowth on land behind the factory of W J Furse, virtually no trace remains today.

In 1969 mechanical signalling also disappeared, with the opening of Trent Power Box. Midland Station's East and West signal boxes, together with London Road Junction were demolished, and the two small platform boxes were converted to stores.

Beeching and beyond

The Sixties saw a progressive decline in the fortunes of the local railway network. As a direct consequence of the 1962 Beeching Report, many local routes served by trains from Midland Station closed. This decade saw an end to Mansfield and Worksop services, and incredibly, direct trains to London (via Melton Mowbray). It almost saw loss of Lincoln services, but these were reprieved at the eleventh hour.

Nottingham Midland Station was renamed Nottingham Station in 1968, following the closure of the Great Central route and Nottingham Victoria. The decade that followed saw the station's fortunes reach their lowest ebb, with shrinking services and reduced passenger numbers. Platform 2 ceased to be used for passenger trains and Platform 6 was abandoned for all but football specials, its connecting steps at the west end of the dispersal bridge being removed. The easternmost blocks of platform buildings were demolished, and the parcels hoists and luggage bridge removed. The avoiding goods lines were removed to the south, and the Queens Road yard was lifted to make way for a car park.

The station's eastern footbridge was removed in around 1985, and the vacated bridge span across the Nottingham Canal was reused to carry steam mains for the City's District Heat scheme. Some investment was made, particularly in a new travel centre and revised ticketing arrangements, but the wider picture was one of decline.

Rock bottom was arguably hit in about 1980, when, against a background of Government indifference to the railways, one business study suggested complete closure of much of the remaining network, including Nottingham Station. Track alignments would be converted to roads, and only the London commuter lines would remain. Fortunately sanity prevailed, and the report was quietly filed away.

Opposite : Two views of the Lincoln mail service taken by the late C A Hill in Nottingham Midland Station during 1957.

Top : Ex GC Director No 62670 "Marne" of Darnall shed stands beneath the luggage bridge at the eastern end of the station. The bridge from Station Street to Queens Road is visible in the background.

Bottom : Ex GE D16 No 62535 is seen with the same diagram on a different occasion, standing in Platform 3. The canopy glazing was replaced with corrugated sheeting after the war, the deep shadow on the platform behind being a direct result.

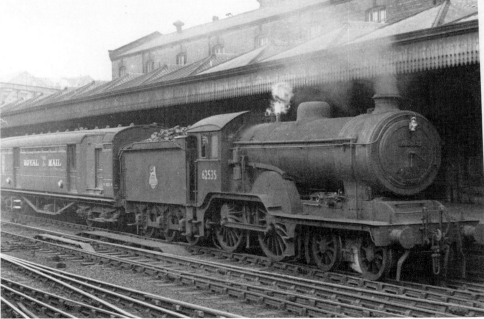

Above : One of the last steam workings into Nottingham Midland was the RCTS East Midlander No 9 Railtour of 21st May 1966. This was worked by Class 9F No 92077, and is seen here by the water column at the west end of Platform 6.

Ronald Askew

Below : A decade later and steam was a distant memory. Through the 1970s and early 1980s, express passenger trains were handled by Class 45 "Peak" locomotives. 45114 and 45001 are seen here at the eastern end of the station on a Bank Holiday Monday in May 1981. A third Peak stood in platform 3 to the right, but the Authors lack of film or wide angle lens unfortunately meant that it went unrecorded.

The fall & rise of Midland Station

By the late 1980s, it was becoming apparent to the City's Transport Planners that continuing growth in car ownership and road transport was unsustainable in an urban environment. Several strategies were evolved to combat the problem, and one of these was to encourage rail travel. Several local authority led schemes improved access links to the station and British Rail and its successors committed money to improving facilities. After initial teething problems in the years following privatisation, train Operators began to improve service provision. This has continued to develop, and with the support of regional development bodies such as EMDA (East Midlands Development Agency), service provision is now better than it has been for decades, and planned signalling improvements are set to deliver further gains in operational performance.

A light rail system was designed during the 1990s to terminate at the station, and this finally opened in March 2004. It was an instant success and its direct connection to rail services has boosted passenger throughput.

The most recent chapter in the revival of the station's fortunes is the Nottingham Station Masterplan, a partnership project between Local Authorities, Network Rail and Train Operating Companies.

The schemes objective is to turn the station into a true transport interchange, improving pedestrian, bus, car, cyclist and taxi access. It will provide better links to an expanded NET light rail system, and create space for a future new platform to the south to cater for expanded train services. The proposals have been designed to be sympathetic to the historic features of the station, including substantial replacement of the corrugated steel on the canopy roofs with glazing, and refurbishment the Porte Cochere entrance and main Booking Hall. Public spaces around the station will be greatly improved, with wider footways leading to better defined entrances.

It is anticipated that the project will become a reality some time after 2010, leaving Nottingham with an attractive revitalised station ready for the demands of the Twenty First Century.

A ticket issued in May 1895 for a journey to Worksop, from the second Midland Station. This journey ceased to be possible in 1964 when the Leen Valley line closed. Services were reinstated however in 1996, with the opening of the Robin Hood Line.

Ian Askew Collection

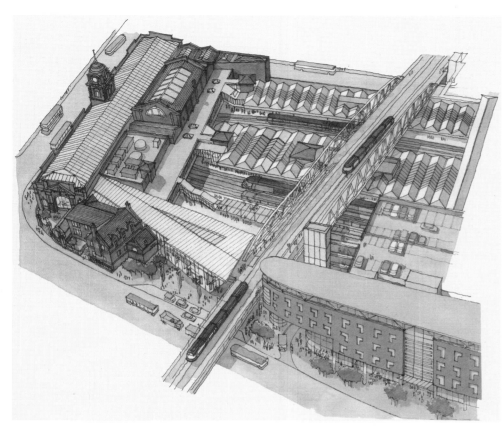

Nottm City Council / BDP

The new Queens Road entrance will have a clean contemporary appearance that will complement rather than compete with the existing architecture.

Manchester based Architects BDP (Building Design Partnership) have developed the design by working closely with the partner organisations. Using experience from developing Manchester Piccadilly, they have produced a design that should enable Nottingham Station to function, not only as a railway station, but as a true transport interchange well into the Twenty First Century.

Above : A partnership of Network Rail, Central Trains, Midland Mainline, the City and County Councils, Nottingham Development Enterprise and the East Midlands Development Agency are promoting redevelopment and improvement of station facilities at Nottingham. Many of the key changes are visible in the artist's impression above. New parking and taxi facilities on Queens Road will link to the existing concourse via an interchange with the Nottingham Express Transit system, which is due to bridge across the station as part of its Phase 2 extension works. Space will be safeguarded beneath the car park for an eventual Platform 7, which will be needed in the next decade or two, if passenger growth matches expectations

The historic fabric of the station is to be conserved as far as possible, and the proposals have been worked up in consultation with English Heritage, and the Rail Heritage Trust.

Nottm City Council / BDP

Right : Part of one of the many survey elevations created by Gleeds Consultants Ltd in order to develop the design is seen here. This view of the south face of the block of buildings on platform 4/5 includes the old south signal box.

Nottm City Council / BDP / Gleeds

Four contemporary views of Nottingham Station taken in February of 2006.

Top left : A Class 170 Unit stands beneath the footbridge in Platform 6 with a Worksop train.

Bottom left : Nottingham Midland South Box was located on platform 4 / 5 and controlled engine movements within the station. It was abolished as a signal box in 1969 and is now used by train crews as a mess room.

Top right : HST services displaced the Peaks from express workings in the early 1980s, and two decades later, they themselves are now being displaced by a new generation of Meridian Units.

Bottom right : A E Lamberts frontage has survived its first century remarkably intact. Under development proposals, the cramped taxi ranks in the Porte Cochere will be replaced by a new facility on Queens Road, allowing the dramatic space inside to be reclaimed for pedestrian use.

In 1868 the site of the original Midland Counties station to the west of Carrington Street was replaced with a bonded goods warehouse. A Class 107 DMU from Derby is seen passing it in 1984. It was demolished a decade later to make way for a new Magistrates Court.

Nottingham MPD was located across the running lines from Wilford Road Goods Depot. Built in 1875, it boasted two roundhouses and a substantial allocation of locomotives. 56100 "Royal Scot" is seen here gently simmering outside the shed in 1962. The Photographers son and friend pose for the picture.

Ronald Askew

By the 1980s much of the goods infrastructure had passed out of use in Nottingham. Yards once stretched almost to Castle Rock. A few sidings were still in place when this 1982 view was recorded, but even these were to be removed, to make way for Inland Revenue offices.

Nottingham Shed was perhaps more readily known for its allocation of six coupled and mixed traffic designs. 2F No 58137 is seen together with an unidentified 3F parked up in 1955. The 3F is clearly out of use, with a tarpaulin covering its funnel.

C A Hill

Nottingham Shed was a favourite haunt of more adventurous local trainspotters. Security was less tight than at Colwick, and the arrangement of Roundhouses, and long boundary with its broken fence allowed the Railway Police to be avoided. 45611 "Hong Kong" is seen resting between duties in one of the roundhouses in the late 1950s.

C A Hill

The yards beyond the sheds often revealed something of interest. 2F No 58175 was a regular performer on local freight workings and it is seen here at rest on a Sunday morning some time during 1957.

C A Hill

Rebuilt Royal Scot 46152 "Kings Dragoon Guardsman" is seen undergoing a piston and valve inspection in the Running Shed in 1957.

C A Hill

On the same day as the above shot, 1F No 41712 was also present in the yard at Nottingham Shed. The open cab design of this class of locomotives harks to a time when little consideration was given to working conditions for the footplate crew.

C A Hill

The original roundhouse at Nottingham was located close to the corner of Station Street and London Road. Jubilee No 45627 "Sierra Leone" of Derby Shed is seen from London Road passing the site of the old roundhouse with a parcels working in about 1960.

E Shelton

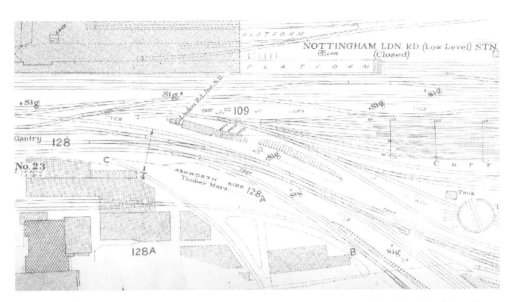

The plan above is an extract from an official layout of the area around London Road Junction. The west end of the carriage sidings and the incoming London lines are clearly visible, together with the rail connection into the City Council's Eastcroft Depot.

Author's Collection

To the east of London Road the lines for London diverged to the south. The GNR terminus was located immediately north and can be seen in the background, as a Class 3MT tank passes with a local passenger service from Lincoln in about 1960.

E Shelton

Beyond London Road Junction lay Nottingham Carriage Sidings. Towards the end of steam these were updated to stable diesel multiple units. The refuelling points are seen in this unattributed view dating from about 1980.

Author's Collection

Sneinton Junction box was located to the eastern end of the carriage sidings, and controlled Meadow Lane crossing, the junction with the exchange yards with the GNR, and the eastern entry to the avoiding freight lines. By 2005 it was merely a crossing box.

In 1988 Meadow Lane was still a through route from Trent Bridge to Sneinton. The level crossing, footbridge and adjacent GNR overbridge are visible in the middle distance on this view. Today this site is occupied by a major road development and the crossing is closed to traffic. The footbridge is gone, and so is the original GNR bridge. The signal box is scheduled to be abolished some time after 2010.

From 1958, Lincoln services were dieselised. This 1967 view from Meadow Lane footbridge records a Cravens Type DMU approaching Sneinton Junction.

C A Hill

The area between the Midland Railway and Meadow Lane was once occupied by the railway engineering works of Thomas Wards, who manufactured track components at the site. It closed in around 1980, and by 1988 the buildings were part demolished ruins.

2. The Great Northern Arrives

2.1 London Road (Low Level)

The Trojan Horse

The earliest of Nottingham's lost lines was the Great Northern Railways route east from London Road (Low Level) Station to Netherfield Junction. The line was born of the rivalry between the Midland and the GNR in the middle part of the nineteenth century, and discarded in the scramble to close lines during the 1960s.

The Midland Railway had a monopoly in the Nottingham area until the arrival of the Ambergate, Nottingham, Boston & East Junction Railway in 1850. This ambitiously named company initially didn't reach any of the destinations in its title. It did however succeed in constructing 22 miles of line from Grantham to Colwick. A junction here with the Midland's line to Lincoln allowed the Ambergate to run trains on Midland metals into Nottingham itself.

All was well until the GNR "Towns Line" arrived at Grantham in 1852. A connection was built to the eastern end of the Ambergate, and the Company signed an agreement with the GNR to operate trains over the line. The GN now had access to the outskirts of Nottingham, although not into the city itself. The company was unlikely to secure an agreement with its arch-rival, the Midland, to run into their station in Nottingham. Nonetheless it proceeded with advertising a new service from London to Nottingham, on the pretence that the locomotive and coaches were hired to the Ambergate, and thus allowed to use Midland metals. A confrontation was inevitable.

Above : A blue Third Class ticket issued by the Great Northern for a journey from London Road Low Level to East Norton, via the LNW Joint Line. This ticket dates from 26th April 1904.

Ian Askew Collection

The Midland were not about to accept the GN's slight of hand, and when the first train from Kings Cross arrived at Nottingham they were ready and waiting. The London train was impounded and the passengers were fined for travelling without a valid ticket. The GN loco crew having uncoupled the train saw the Midland staff closing in and attempted to make a break for it with their engine.

London Road in 1957. Passenger services had finished more than a decade before, and the station was being used for storage of stock. The yard beyond was still busy, and continued to be so for some years to come.

C A Hill

Running around the now stranded train, they found their path blocked by a strategically placed Midland loco. Several other engines swiftly converged on them and now trapped, the crew were dragged off their mount, which was hauled away and locked in a disused shed. The rails to this were lifted, and there it remained for seven months whilst legal proceedings rumbled on.

A New Station

Following this incident, it became clear that the Ambergate could not continue to take access to Midland metals on satisfactory terms, and retain its association with the Great Northern. In 1853 the Company's board of Directors sanctioned construction of a new twin track line from Colwick into Nottingham, paralleling the Midland route. The new line was to terminate at a major new station near Eastcroft Hall, alongside what was then called Flood Road. Parliamentary powers were obtained in 1854, and construction began shortly after. The construction of the Railway included a deal with the Nottingham Corporation to upgrade part of Flood Road, now renamed London Road to reflect its increased importance. The new station , was ultimately to take the same name (although it was initially called simply "Nottingham"), and it opened its doors to passengers in 1857.

The train shed is seen in 1990, when much of the site had been cleared, and the old station was struggling to find a new use. During its conversion to a health spa and fitness club, the roof and glazing was stripped off and renewed, allowing modern insulation materials to be incorporated into the structure. The signalling store (originally a goods shed) stood in the foreground and was demolished in the mid 1980s. The chimney of Eastcroft Incinerator is visible in the background.

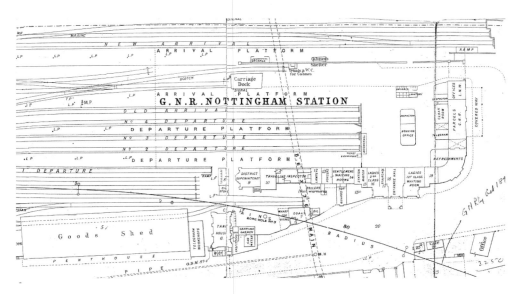

Above : Extract from GNR plans of 1895, prepared for the GNR Act of the same year, relating to a projected connection with the planned GCR London Extension. The station was still named "Nottingham" at this time. The goods shed shown was used by the LNWR briefly, and was latterly used as signalling stores. The alignment shown on the plan for the new line would have involved a level crossing on London Road. Fortunately this option was not taken forward, and the link was subsequently developed as a high level line, opening in 1899.

Ian Trivett Collection

Below : Elevation of the main buildings at London Road in their final condition. The station essentially survives externally as shown, but with the addition of glazing to fully enclose the train shed. The entire complex has been converted into a fitness centre, and looks to have a more secure future than at any time in the past quarter-century.

Courtesy of Greenhatch Building Surveys Ltd

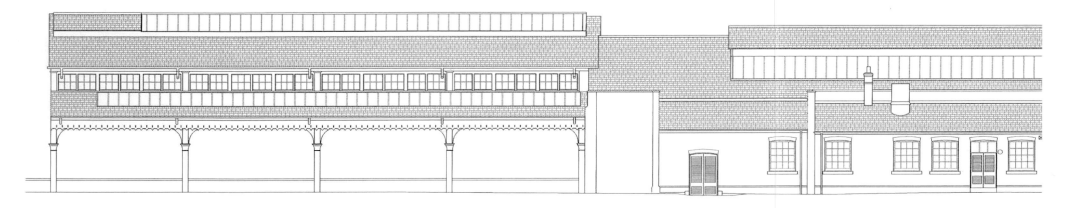

Designed by local architect T C Hine, the Gothic frontage was elegant and imposing, and included a covered carriage entrance. Behind the buildings, a three span wrought-iron train shed protected the bay platforms from the elements. There were only two platforms initially, but additional ones were added as traffic grew. Facilities at London Road were comprehensive. The striking two-storey goods warehouse with its circular windows and large arches incorporated hydraulic hoists to lift wagons to the upper floor. The ground floor was kept clear for goods in this unusual building, by suspending the first floor from the roof structure with iron tie rods.

There were facilities for interchange of goods with the Nottingham Canal, and extensive stables for horses. Iron horses were catered for with a two road shed, turntable, coaling stage and watering facilities.

In 1861 the Ambergate amalgamated with the Great Northern, and the latter Company assumed effective responsibility for all aspects of operating the line. Goods facilities at London Road were expanded. Exchange roads with the Midland Railway were provided, and sidings were built to serve the new Nottingham Corporation Gas works. The engine shed would close when the new GN depot at Colwick opened in 1887, but goods traffic remained important at London Road for years to come. Passenger traffic grew quickly during the first twenty years and the main station was upgraded in the 1880s, and the platforms reorganised and train shed extended to cater for the longer trains that were using the station.

The station buildings are seen here in around 1990, when they had fallen into neglect. The windows had been broken by vandals and the building's future looked uncertain.

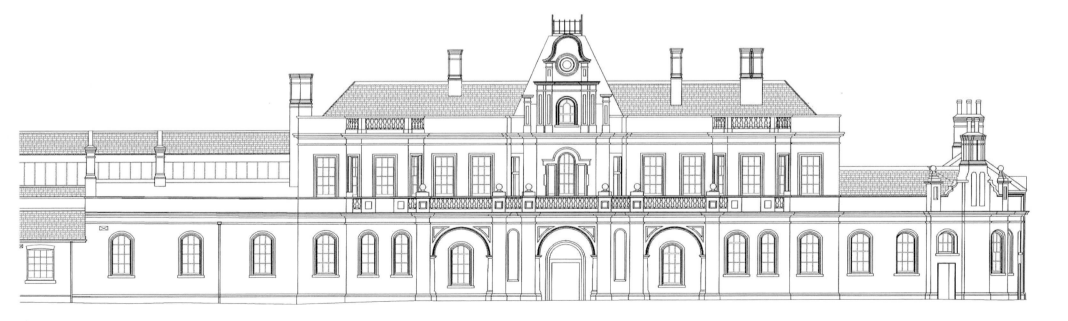

Above : Side elevation of London Road station. Note the awning is omitted for clarity. The elevated block on the right is a later addition to the original building.

Courtesy Greenhatch Building Surveys Ltd

Above : Low Level Station is seen here in 1957, before its conversion to a parcels concentration depot. The station was little altered from pre-grouping days at this time, but already starting to look shabby.

C A Hill

Arrival of the LNWR

From 1875, London & North Western Railway passenger trains from Northampton began using the station, running in with the GN's agreement from the new joint line through the Vale of Belvior, via Saxondale Junction. The Company initially leased a single storey timber goods warehouse at London Road from the GN, but in 1882 it constructed its own extensive goods warehouse and sidings to the north side of Manvers Street. The yard was built on an elevated sandstone outcrop and a two storey four road goods shed provided. Beneath this the company quarried away the rock to construct a further underground warehouse. This was used for many years by Fyffes as a distribution depot for fruit delivered by rail. The yard was accessed by a short double track line constructed from a junction at Trent Lane, a mile to the east of London Road. This link was noteworthy as the shortest distinct line on the entire LNW network, measuring a mere 20 chains in length.

Decline, Enemy Action and new directions

When Victoria Station opened, most passenger services transferred away from London Road. This was renamed "Low Level" to avoid confusion with the new "High Level" station on the adjacent viaduct that connected to the Great Central. The LNWR were unable to secure an agreement with the GCR to use Victoria, so their trains continued to use the old terminus, together with occasional specials.

During the First World War the station was used for ambulance trains, and repatriated wounded from the Western Front (including the Author's Great Grandfather) were received here. On the night of 23rd September 1916 Nottingham was attacked by Zeppelins and the railways were singled out for attention. The flight of seven airships, deprived of navigational aids by the blackout, struggled to find their target. L17 was the only one to meet with any success, following the lights of a train heading west from Grantham. A number of bombs were dropped and several civilians were killed, but the railway escaped serious damage.

The Second World War found new roles for Low Level Station. The offices were used as Operations headquarters for the coordination of freight movements across the East Midlands. The area was again bombed on 8/9 May 1941, this time with appreciable damage to the GN and adjacent Midland yards. Windows were blown out and the roof damaged on the Goods Yard signal box, tracks were badly damaged and rolling stock destroyed. The LNWR warehouse at Manvers Street was burned out after direct hits. Casualties were high with the raid costing the lives of over 200 people, including 49 in a single hit on the Coop Bakery on Meadow Lane.

Above : The Goods Yard Box was one of two signal boxes controlling London Road Low Level. Seen here in 1981, it was the last survivor and still in use as a shunting frame. Note the small armed somersault signals beyond the box. These were the last of the type in the area, and were removed to York museum after they ended their working days.

Left : A 1981 view from the station entrance, through the finely proportioned portico towards the later High Level Station, and the Island Site works of Jesse Boot beyond. Nothing of the view beyond the portico now exists.

There were many unusual workings to the station at this time, including prisoner of war trains. The strain put on the system by wartime operating conditions however meant the writing was on the wall for regular passenger services. The station closed its doors to the public in 1944, and the LNW services transferred to Victoria. After a spell in use as railway offices and a storage facility for stock, the station was converted into a parcels concentration depot in 1962.

Conversion of the station into a parcels depot included filling the northern bay platform in and panelling off the end span of the train shed. A new canopy was provided on Platform 1 and a concrete apron built for road vehicles. The signals store is just visible to the right and the base of a capstan for cable shunting is to the right of the pile of sleepers.

Manvers Street Goods Yard closed completely in the mid sixties and all traces of the depot and connecting lines were swiftly removed, to be replaced by a housing estate and a scrapyard. The subterranean warehouse survived however in private use, and still exists at the time of writing

London Road Parcels Depot, together with the sidings, warehouses and signal engineers stores continued to be busy for nearly two more decades. The 1882 Goods Yard signal box remained open for shunting movements, and the last Great Northern somersault signals in the area could still be found at work here as late as 1982 (the last ones being removed to the National Railway Museum). A single line remained in situ to the abandoned Trent Lane junction. This continued in use until 1974 as a headshunt for reversing gypsum trains from Hotchley Hill on the GCR, and into the 1980s for the occasional shunting movement from the yard.

A view taken from a first floor window, looking down the southern span of the train shed. Parcels operations were in the process of winding up, and the rows of trolleys seen on the platforms would soon be redundant. The ties and struts of the wrought iron roof trusses and cast iron columns are shown to good effect in this view. Today keep fit enthusiasts pay to exercise here, where porters once toiled to load heavy parcels.

The 1980s saw the London Road site in terminal decline. The parcels depot closed in 1981, and the signal stores in the old timber goods shed followed a couple of years after. The sidings remained in use for engineers stock, but these too were progressively abandoned. By the end of the decade, the now disused station was boarded up and the abandoned Goods Yard box derelict and vandalised. The goods sheds continued to be occupied and were reasonably well maintained, but the tracks had gone and rail use had finally come to an end after 130 years. Ownership transferred to the City Council.

New uses for old assets

In 1990 a new road into the city cut through the site, and the small yard buildings and cattle dock, together with the viaduct leading to High Level Station and Weekday Cross were demolished. The eastern half of the yard was redeveloped for housing, and the route from the new road to Trent Lane was converted into a green corridor and recreational walk. The bridge carrying the route to Victoria over Meadow Lane was demolished, and the 1856 wrought iron bridge (Bridge 45) was replaced with a second hand steel one, the original deck having been badly damaged by an over-height vehicle.

The goods sheds took longer to be rescued. The shell of the original building lapsed into a ruinous state (an application for its demolition was rejected in the late nineties on the grounds of its listed status). The history of this structure took on a grim aspect in early 2005, when it was the site of two murders.

The newer "James Alexander" building retained continuous occupation, by an antiques dealer and a fitted kitchen retailer. Its exterior presented a dilapidated appearance but inside, those floors undamaged by the 1993 fire remained surprisingly well preserved and many original interior fittings remained, including enamelled British Railways "No Smoking" notices.

The grain and goods warehouse built at the turn of the century is seen here with Engineer's stock in 1981. The warehouses are now destined to become apartments.

The timber Refreshment Room in the north east corner of the train shed is seen in this 1981 view. The curved ironwork of the roof above is an unusual feature.

Efforts were made by the City Council to find a new use for the old station, which by now had listed status. A transport museum was proposed at one stage but support was not forthcoming and the empty building was progressively vandalised. The two brick built goods sheds faired worse still, and in 1992 the original 1857 building was completely gutted by fire, just four years after the roof had been renewed. The historic wagon lifts and suspended floor construction were totally destroyed, and the masonry badly damaged.

The 1880s goods shed also suffered extensive fire damage in 1993, and again in 2005, with the roof and upper storey being destroyed.

The vandalised remains of the Goods Yard signal box were dismantled in 1991 by enthusiasts, with a view to possible preservation. Some elements were removed to the Nottingham Transport Heritage Centre for potential reuse, but the structure had deteriorated through years of neglect and exposure to the elements. British Rail had already removed anything of value when the box closed, and other than the lever frame, little was eventually salvaged.

London Road Low Level's future was finally secured in 1999, when the station was sold for development into a health spa and fitness centre. The Developer restored the original fabric of the building, and the train shed was sympathetically converted, retaining much of its original appearance.

The site occupied by the two warehouses fell within an area that the City Council was keen to see redeveloped. In 2005 a Planning Application was approved for reconstruction of the warehouses as apartments, and conversion work began in 2006. Unfortunately little of the remaining internal fabric will be suitable for reuse, but the exteriors of the buildings are to be tastefully restored, and missing roofs replaced. In time the former warehouses will become desirable and well appointed residential properties, overlooking an attractive lake feature and accessed by tree lined avenues and walkways. This will be far replaced from the soot encrusted warehousing that once overlooked the Gasworks and railway yards.

A NET light rail connection to the site is even under consideration.

Above : The interior of the refreshment room in Low Level Station seen in 1981, showing the attention to detail paid to the woodwork during its construction.

Below : The Goods Yard Box, again viewed in 1981. The locking room windows were bricked up as a precaution against bomb damage in the Second World War. The extension on the right hand side is an unusual feature.

A view east towards Trent Lane Junction from Bridge No 45 over Meadow Lane in 1967. The deck of this bridge was widened and then reduced in width during its life, before final replacement in the 1990s.

C A Hill

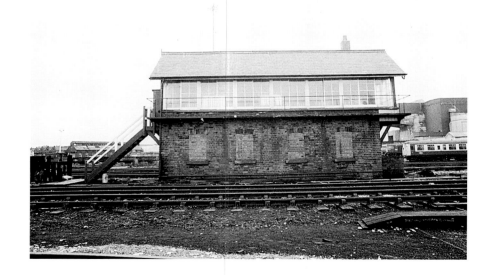

Top : London Road (Low Level) Station in 1957. The vehicle nearest the camera is of LMS origin.
C A Hill

Bottom : Low Level Station is obscured by the smog in this 1957 photograph. The level difference between the GNR and Midland lines is apparent.
C A Hill

Left : The signalling stores and goods offices were located to the north of the station platforms. They are seen here in 1981, towards the end of their working lives.

Top : The original 1857 warehouses are seen here, together with Engineers Department stock and parcels vehicles in 1981. This historic structure was gutted by fire in 1992.

Bottom : The 'James Alexander' warehouse was built at the same time as the line into Victoria. The yards were substantially reorganised and facilities updated. This building was also fire damaged after it passed out of railway use.

Right : Detail shot of an 1857 loading hoist. Note the elaborate cast iron bracket supporting the structure. This detail was lost in the 1992 fire.

Above : In 1991 the County Council began construction of a road through the east of the yard. By this time the tracks had gone, the Goods Yard Box was a vandalised shell and the warehouses were in use for, amongst other things, paint storage and antique shipping.

Below The catastrophic fire of 1992 rendered the original warehouse a complete ruin. Pictured here 14 years after, it was still awaiting rescue.

Above : The pump house and its distinctive tank were still in moderate condition in 2006, when work began on conversion into apartments.

Below : A reminder of railway days. The rollers provided on each external corner of the building were to facilitate shunting of wagons with capstans and hawsers. Grooves are still visible from the wear of the cables.

2.2 East to Netherfield & Colwick

The GN built only one intermediate station on the route from Colwick, this being Racecourse Station. It was built some 30 years after the line opened, and sited as its name suggests, adjacent to the Nottingham Racecourse, a short way east of Trent Lane Junction. This station was little more than a halt, with timber shelters provided on the two platforms and a signal box beyond the western end of the up platform. This was only used at busy times, and was mostly closed out. No direct connection was provided between the two platforms, and passengers crossed over the line by means of ramps from the platforms down to Racecourse Road. A goods dock was provided to east of the Colwick Road overbridge (The Hall Sidings) but facilities here were minimal. Other than race specials, few trains used the station. It closed in 1955.

An unidentified J6 departs Netherfield & Colwick with a Nottingham Train in 1959. The station was rebuilt shortly after, and a new signal box constructed immediately behind the engine's position.

C A Hill

B1 No 61056 passes the Hall Signal Box with the 2.18 pm Nottingham to Grantham train on 1st March 1955. The photographer notes that this working was 40 minutes late due to a derailment at Nottm Victoria South Box.

N(B)MRS / D R Morley

The next station to be reached, and the only GNR built station in Nottingham to remain open today was Netherfield & Colwick. Built in 1878, it was situated immediately to the west of the Derbyshire Extension's connection at Colwick West Junction. The station was configured as a single island platform, with access from an overbridge by means of steps. The range of single storey timber and brick buildings on the platform was typical of GNR commuter stations, and canopies covered both platform faces. An unusual feature of the station was the incorporation of a signal box into the buildings, to control access to the Derbyshire Extension line.

This box was abolished in 1961 and replaced with a new structure to the west of the overbridge. The station itself was rebuilt shortly afterwards, and other than the platform, little remains of the original station today.

Trent Lane Junction was revised in 1886, with the arrival of the Nottingham Suburban Railway. The Suburban up line crossed the GNR tracks at a high level on two highly skewed bowstring girder spans before joining the GN, whilst the down line peeled away sharply to the north immediately after the Trent Lane overbridge. At the GNR's insistence, one of the Suburban line spans was constructed of sufficiently long to allow future widening of their line to four tracks.

Further expansion at the junction came in 1899 with the construction of the high level avoiding line into Nottingham Victoria. Trent Lane effectively became the focus of four separate railways, all converging above the original Midland line.

The commencement of construction of the link from Trent Lane to Victoria in 1897 provided the GN with an opportunity to remodel and upgrade its goods facilities. The sidings serving the Corporation Gasworks were realigned, the layout of the north east corner of the yard revised and more importantly, a new grain warehouse constructed immediately east of T C Hine's original. With these changes, goods facilities reached their zenith at London Road, and in the months before Victoria opened, the combination of goods and passenger traffic made it a very busy place indeed.

Ex Great Eastern Class J69/1 No 68554 is seen at Netherfield & Colwick in 1959 with a Permanent Way train. The ex GCR brake van is of interest.

C A Hill

The latter half of the Twentieth Century saw decline and closure. Trent Lane junction was rationalised in 1954. The now severed Suburban Railway connections were lifted. The twin span bowstring flyover was removed and the redundant formation abandoned.

Following the closure of Nottingham Victoria in September 1967, the network of local lines was dramatically cut back. The original connection between the old Ambergate line and the Midland at Colwick had been reinstated in 1964 allowing the Grantham service (originally earmarked for closure by Beeching) to transfer to Nottingham Midland. It had taken nearly 120 years for the wheel to come full circle. The duplicate GN route remained open for dwindling Colwick freights, but these finished in 1969 and the line closed to the east of Trent Lane junction.

End of the line

The three wrought iron spans of the grimly named Sludge Bank Bridge (Bridge 43) to the west of Racecourse Station were demolished soon after closure of the through route. The three span deck of Trent Lane overbridge (Bridge 44) was removed in 1984, and the area of land to each side of Trent Lane Junction was cleared of much of the remaining railway infrastructure.

The route east to Colwick lay derelict for some years before development obliterated the formation. In 1983 the County Council constructed a new road along the route from just west of Mile End Road to Racecourse Road. In the process of this, Colwick Road overbridge (Bridge 42) was demolished, together with the nearby abutments of the earlier 1857 bridge that it had replaced. The access ramp and platform remains at Racecourse Station were also removed, along with the abandoned GNR concrete signal posts and the remaining east abutment of Bridge 43. Surprisingly the loading dock for The Hall sidings was left in place, and this is just visible today at the back of the grass verge on the A612.

Further east, the remainder of the alignment has been gradually claimed by housing developments. Today nothing remains.

Boundary marker for the division between Eastern and Midland Regions, to the west of Netherfield & Colwick. Photographed in August 1955.

N(B)MRS / D R Morley

Postscript

The Nottingham (Bulwell) Model Railway Society has recreated the complexity of Trent Lane Junction in miniature. Parts of this '00' Scale model were displayed for the first time at the Nottingham East Midlands Model Railway Exhibition on the 150th anniversary of the opening of the GNR route in 2007. Subsequent appearances at exhibitions around the country will allow many thousands of people to experience how the busy junction would have appeared in its heyday.

There were three principal bridges between Nottingham and Colwick on the original line. Bridges on the route numbered from the Grantham end of the line.

Above : Bridge No 45 was a wrought iron structure with cast iron parapets and a 25 foot span. It was extended in 1876 and again in 1888, with the original deck being reconstructed in 1903. The photo comes from the GNR Engineers office and dates from 1903. *Author's Collection*

Below : Bridge No 44 comprised three spans, with plate girder main beams. It is seen here in 1972. *C A Hill*

Above : Bridge 43 is referred to in the District Engineer's records as "Sludge Bank Bridge". It comprised three spans of 55', 30' and 29'. It was reconstructed in the form seen here in 1893. To the right, an access ramp led to Racecourse Station, and Company posters can be seen on the wing wall. The Midland's Colwick Crossing box is visible in the background. *Author's Collection*

Below : On the 1st March 1955 an unidentified Austerity is seen with an Up Goods to the east of The Hall Sidings. The footbridge also spanned the adjacent Midland tracks.

N(B)MRS / D R Morley

Bridge No 42 is recorded here by the Official Photographer on the 12th March 1903, by which time it clearly needed a coat of paint. This structure had wrought iron plate girders, and corrugated decking. The length of the span was 51 feet and three inches. It was demolished by the LNER, to be replaced with a skew twin span steel structure immediately to the east.

Author's Collection

Top : Looking east from Trent Lane Junction, past the Suburban Line flyover in 1975.

C A Hill

Above : The same area seen some eight years later, looking west, after removal of the tracks. Today this area is completely overgrown, and the abutments of the flyover virtually invisible.

Left : A GNR concrete signal post stands sentinel at the truncated end of the formation near the site of Bridge 43 in 1984. The A612 Colwick Loop Road can be seen in the distance, following the old railway alignment.

Top : The deck of Bridge 44 is seen here in 1983. The tracks have been lifted, and the timbering covering the cross beams is exposed. The four waybeams that supported the rails can be seen.

Above : Bridge 42 is seen just prior to its demolition. It replaced an earlier wrought iron structure (see page 31) that had been built to provide access to Colwick Hall. The north abutment of the old bridge remained in place until 1983, when it was reduced to the pile of rubble seen in the foreground, during construction of the Colwick Loop Road.

Right : Trains rejoin the metals of the Ambergate / Great Northern at Netherfield Junction. The last semaphore signal under control of Netherfield Junction (No 28) is seen here in June 2005. The old Stationmasters house, with its distinctive barge boards can be seen in the background.

Netherfield Junction Signal Box was built in 1960, and replaced the original box that was incorporated into the station buildings. It controlled the newly laid connection to the Midland line, and access to the spur of the old Back Line that led to Gedling Colliery. The closure of the GN line into Nottingham in 1969 resulted in a simpler junction layout at Netherfield.

Above : In 1954, LNER platform tickets were still being issued at Netherfield & Colwick Station, six years after nationalisation.

Author's Collection

The somewhat claustrophobic interior of Netherfield Junction Box is seen here in June 2005. The Railway Signalling Company frame was second-hand when installed, and doubtless came from a redundant box in the area.

3. Colwick : Steam Sheds and Sidings.

The Railway comes to Colwick

The origins of the railway yards at Colwick date back to the construction of the Ambergate, Nottingham, Boston and Eastern Junction Railway in 1850. This independent company constructed a facility on the site of what was to become Colwick Yard, at the end of Netherfield Lane, by Carlton Fields Farm. This somewhat remote outpost was intended to handle freight traffic from Grantham. Commercial rivalry however between its business partner, the Great Northern, and the Midland Railway led to the focussing of all operations here, including passenger services, when access to Nottingham via Midland metals was blocked in 1852 (see Chapter 2).

The Ambergate built its own line in to Nottingham from Colwick in 1857, and provided improved freight facilities on the City's outskirts at London Road, together with a small locomotive depot. Space here was restricted, and as traffic grew, the depot became increasingly unsatisfactory. In 1862 the Ambergate amalgamated with the Great Northern. The GN had plans for expansion, and these led to the search for a new site for a larger depot. A site by the original yard at Colwick was selected, alongside the Company's new Derbyshire Extension line, and the first depot was built there in 1875. The shed had four roads, and outbuildings where small maintenance operations could be undertaken.

The opening of the depot coincided with the commencement of services over the Derbyshire Extension, which left the Grantham line at Netherfield and turned north (the portion of this route to Basford came to be known locally as "The Back Line") A second chord was built from the Derbyshire Extension to the Grantham line, further towards the River Trent, creating a triangle. The junctions at each apex were Colwick North Junction, Colwick East Junction and Netherfield Junction in the west.

The depot was located within the triangle, and faced north, with the outlet by Colwick North Junction.

Coal was the driving force behind the Derbyshire Extension. Collieries served by the network of connecting lines, were to generate a huge volume of traffic. The GNR selected the Colwick triangle as a suitable location to lay reception sidings for this new coal traffic, and the first yard was laid in 1875, whilst the shed was under construction.

Expansion

Coal traffic from the Erewash and Leen Valleys steadily expanded, and iron ore traffic grew, following the opening of the GN / LNW Joint railway and improved access to the ironstone quarries of the Vale of Belvoir. It soon became necessary to remodel and expand the yards.

In 1891 the eastern side of the Colwick triangle was realigned, with a new junction created by the River Trent (Rectory Junction). The direction of Colwick East junction was reversed, to create an outlet for engines from the reception sidings. The extra space within the triangle, together with land to the east of the old main line was used to lay additional sidings. The final layout comprised five principal yards, with reception sidings at the northern and eastern ends. Total capacity was in excess of 6000 wagons.

During the period of freight growth, the depot was progressively expanded to cope with the extra demand for locomotives. The original 1875 shed was extended in 1882 with an eight road shed being added alongside. The two became known respectively as the Small and Large Sheds, and the enlarged depot had capacity for 250 locomotives. A large repair shop was also built, allowing the depot to undertake heavy repair work. Construction was not just limited to locomotive servicing facilities however. Extensive offices were built, together with messing facilities for crews. Rows of railway owned terrace housing were built, and even a railwayman's institute.

Colwick Shed had a strong allocation of ex Great Central classes for many years. Robinson J11 No 64392 is seen in 1958, standing over one of the inspection pits. It was withdrawn from service at the end of 1958. One of the Shed's J50s stands to the rear.

C A Hill

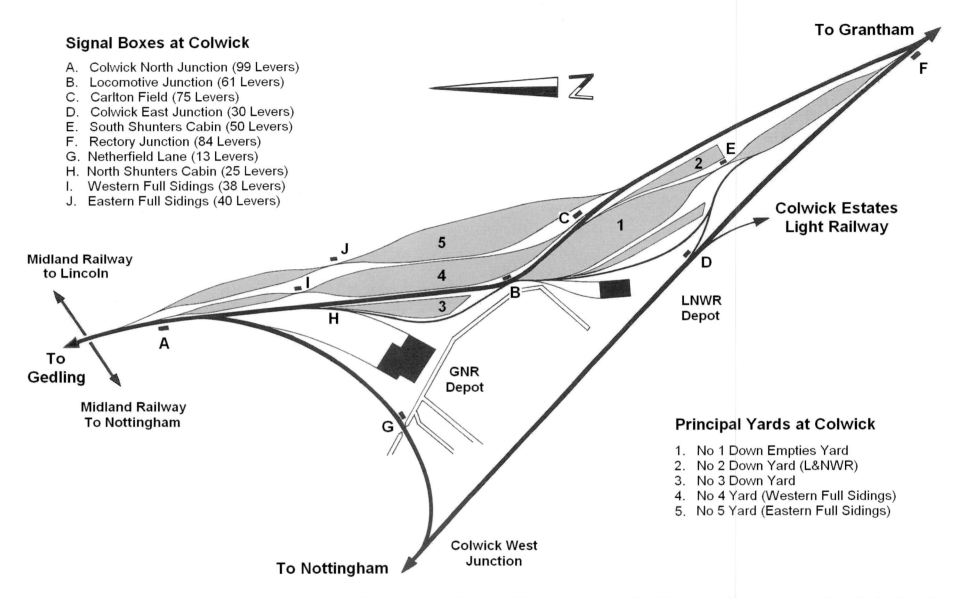

Signal Boxes at Colwick

A. Colwick North Junction (99 Levers)
B. Locomotive Junction (61 Levers)
C. Carlton Field (75 Levers)
D. Colwick East Junction (30 Levers)
E. South Shunters Cabin (50 Levers)
F. Rectory Junction (84 Levers)
G. Netherfield Lane (13 Levers)
H. North Shunters Cabin (25 Levers)
I. Western Full Sidings (38 Levers)
J. Eastern Full Sidings (40 Levers)

To Grantham

F

E

2

C

1

**Colwick Estates
Light Railway**

5

J

D

**Midland Railway
to Lincoln**

4

I

**LNWR
Depot**

3

B

H

A

**To
Gedling**

**Midland Railway
To Nottingham**

**GNR
Depot**

G

Principal Yards at Colwick

1. No 1 Down Empties Yard
2. No 2 Down Yard (L&NWR)
3. No 3 Down Yard
4. No 4 Yard (Western Full Sidings)
5. No 5 Yard (Eastern Full Sidings)

To Nottingham

**Colwick West
Junction**

Above : Schematic view of Colwick Yards and Sheds in their heyday. There were eventually a total of five separate yards, with additional reception and storage sidings. Engine lines allowed light engines released from the yard to go on to the depot. Both GNR and LNWR sheds are shown, although the latter was closed by the LMS in 1928. Appendix 2 contains whiiste signals used by locomotives conducting movements in the yards.

Today, all that remains of this huge complex are the rusting and overgrown remains of No 1 Yard's reception sidings (known as "Spike Bank", a short section of the 1882 main line deviation, which serves an oil terminal, Rectory Junction Signal Box and the western side of the triangle from Netherfield Junction. This single line route served Gedling Colliery until it closed, and is now mothballed and overgrown.

In 1881, following the construction of the joint line with the LNWR, the latter company built its own shed in the Colwick triangle, alongside the Grantham line. Access to this eight road northlight shed was taken from Locomotive Junction, to the western end of No 1 Yard. Like the neighbouring GN shed, its allocation was primarily eight coupled freight locomotives for hauling the long coal and iron ore trains that were marshalled in the adjacent yards.

1900-1950 the Peak Years

Colwick was placed in a unique position geographically. The convergence of coal and iron ore traffic from such a large catchment area had led to the creation of the largest complex of its kind in Europe. The demand for locomotives to haul the freight had resulted in the construction of the largest shed on the GNR. The army of personnel needed to make all this work had led to the construction virtually overnight of the railway town of Netherfield.

The investment in Colwick did not end with the GNR. Its successor, in 1936 the LNER built a modern coaling tower (nicknamed the Cenotaph) and supplemented the original 50 foot turntable with a seventy foot vacuum operated example. It even constructed fuel oil tanks, when oil firing was under consideration during the Second World War, although these were never actually used. The yards were updated to reflect changing demand, and much of the site was resignalled with modern upper quadrant signals in the 1930s.

English Electric 400HP shunter No D3629 is seen marshalling a tanker train on the main line by Colwick East Junction in 1959. This was one of seven allocated to the shed, and replaced the J50 and J52 classes previously used for shunting and trip duties. The old LNWR northlight engine shed building is visible in the background. By this time it was in industrial use. The concrete posts of the somersault signals date them to roughly between 1915 and 1925. Many somersaults at Colwick were replaced by the LNER with upper quadrant Westinghouse types.

C A Hill

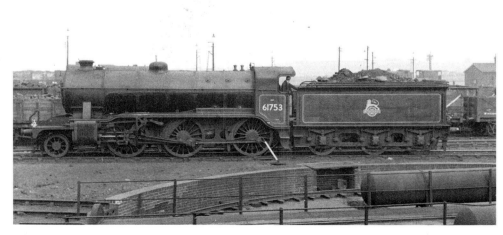

Gresley K2s had a long association with Colwick. It received its first allocation in 1912, and the final withdrawals took place almost half a century later in 1961. 61753 is seen standing by the LNER installed vacuum operated turntable in 1956.

C A Hill

The LMS, by comparison had less enthusiasm in Colwick as a depot site. It inherited the joint line operations that the LNW had built up, but viewed the LNW shed at Colwick was seen as an unnecessary asset. It was closed completely in 1928. Stabling of the locomotives was initially transferred to the GN shed under agreement with the LNER, and the redundant depot given over to wagon storage. It was eventually sold out of rail use altogether.

were carried out after 1958. Consequently many locos had badly worn wheels, which adversely affected their performance.

By the end of the 1950s it was not uncommon for trains ascending the 1 in 100 through Gedling to lose traction in wet conditions and in extreme cases come to a standstill. The Author knew a fireman based at Colwick in the late 1950s, who worked many a freight turn bound for the Leen valley. He recalled that following the end of wheel turning, the condition of the engines notably deteriorated.

On one memorable occasion a particularly decrepit ex Great Central class 04 was tasked with lifting a rake of empties up the Back Line to one of the Leen Valley pits. The loco was in a particularly poor state, and despite the crew's best efforts the train slid to a halt mid-way through Mapperley Tunnel. The hard working engine had filled the bore with smoke and the crew had to tie their handkerchiefs over their faces to prevent choking.

Thompson L1 No 67760 is seen on Shed in 1956. Other identifiable types include a J39 with an ex NER tender, a couple of Austerities and a Robinson Class 04. These classes of locomotive were typical of Colwick's allocation in the post-war years. In the final decade of operation at Colwick, they would be supplanted first by LMS types, then finally by diesels.

C A Hill

The GN facilities at Colwick continued to be an important hub of the railway network even after nationalisation in 1948. The depot was one of the largest on the new Eastern Region, and the yards were still stacked with wagons well into the 1950. All appeared well, but lack of investment and inter-regional rivalry began to take their toll.

Decade of Decline

Restructuring within the Eastern Region, and Colwick Shed's status change from principle district depot to sub-shed of Lincoln seems to have marked the start of the end. In 1958 Colwick Shed's classification was changed from 38A to 40E. Policy regarding routine maintenance of locomotives appears to have changed at the same time. The depot had comprehensive overhaul facilities, including lathes for wheel turning. It had been customary to service locos routinely and ensure that the tyres on the wheels had the correct profile. Anecdotal evidence from former enginemen suggests that this practice was dropped, and only essential repairs

Colwick depot is seen in the twilight of its existence in April 1966. The depot was now controlled by the London Midland Region. LNER designs, Pre-Grouping locomotive types and even the Austerities were long gone. Stanier 8Fs were the principal class now to work out of the depot, together with the odd BR Standard Class 4.

Ronald Askew

The Fireman had the unenviable task of picking his way back on foot along several hundred yards of smoke filled tunnel, along the uneven ballast in pitch dark, trusting that there were no open drainage pits in the cess, before reaching the south entrance. After a hike back along the cutting he reached the telephone point and called the nearest signal box, who summoned a rescue engine from Colwick to bank the stranded train out of the tunnel, to the summit at Arno Vale.

Other crews suffered similar misfortune, but despite representations to the shed's Foreman nothing was done to improve the condition of the allocation and a request for routine attachment of a banking engine to ascending trains was declined. Another notable trip, again with another decrepit eight-coupled type saw a buffer fall off the locomotive somewhere along the Back Line.

Closure of the Back line and Mapperley Tunnel by its new London Midland Region managers resolved the problem with the gradient in 1960. This also severed access to Colwick Yards, and much of the traffic was rerouted to the LMR's rival yard at Toton. A reduction of throughput in the yard meant that fewer locomotives were required. Colwick's dwindling fleet of ailing freight locos soldiered on working less onerous routes, until the final regular steam working out of the depot finished on the last day of 1966.

A dismal view of Colwick is recorded here on 21st February 1967. The only locomotives to be seen are those awaiting the cutter's torch. 8F No 44847 is nearest the camera, with 48603, 48143, 48388, 45289, 45224, 48672, 44941, 48370, 48651 and 48662 in company. The road they stand on was once the engine line avoiding No 3 Yard. By the time the picture was taken, it was storage for scrap metal, and No 3 Yard itself had been lifted. The now redundant coaling tower is visible in the distance.

Ronald Askew

The depot had transferred to Midland Region control the previous year, and with the change of region came a new allocation code (16B). Diesel fuelling facilities were provided, and the depot now housed diesel locomotives, ranging from 350HP Type 1 diesel mechanicals for local freight duties through to main line Type 4 main line diesel electrics.

Local traffic was in terminal decline however, and the closure of the GC and Derbyshire extension routes in 1968 were the final nails in the coffin for Colwick. Most of the freight had already transferred to former Midland metals, and Toton yard became the sole focus for area freight operations. The yards and depot at Colwick closed in 1970, and the Railway Town of Netherfield lost its single biggest employer.

The sidings were not immediately lifted, and continued to be used for the storage of redundant stock for another year or so. The sheds were levelled in 1971, and the coaling tower destroyed by explosives.

Today the site of the depot is occupied by industrial and retail units, and the A612 crosses the site of the loco workshops. The former Railwayman's canteen survives as a social club, whilst the old club house stands empty. Other than this, little is left of one of the country's largest locomotive depots.

The last of the sidings were cleared at the same time as the depot. The exceptions were the reception sidings to No 1 yard, the avoiding engine lines and a section of the old main line left in-situ to serve an oil terminal. Rectory Junction signal box at the southern outlet from the yard also remained to control access to these lines, together with the Cotgrave Colliery branch.

Today only the oil terminal is in use, the other lines being abandoned and overgrown. Rectory Junction box remains open for the time being, but it is unlikely to have a long term future with resignalling of the Nottingham area scheduled for after 2010.

Above : Smoke box door shed plate. Colwick Depot was allocated the code 40E between 1958 and 1965.

Colwick Yards after-closure

Top Left : A Class 170 passes Rectory Junction Box in June 2005 with a train from Grantham. At the time of writing, Rectory Junction is the only GNR built box surviving at Colwick. It dates from the 1882 realignment of the eastern leg of the Colwick triangle and is classified as a GNR Type 1 design. Only a handful of the original 84 levers are now in use.

The nearest lines lead to the oil terminal on the site of the old main lines. The next line across once led into the No 1 Yard reception sidings, but now serves as a cripple road for defective rolling stock.

Bottom Left. Beyond the cripple road, the reception sidings are still largely in place. In January 1999 they were overgrown, and the sleepers deteriorating, but they were surprisingly intact after 30 years of abandonment.

Above : The only active rail use at Colwick today is the supply of oil to the terminal sited on the old main line, not far from where Carlton Fields Signal Box stood. A public right of way crossed the site near to Colwick East Junction, and then passed beneath a pair of brick arched bridges. The more northerly of these is seen in January 1999, with a rake of 100 tonne tankers sat on the old down line.

Above : The remains of a ground frame at the western end of Spike Bank in January 1999. This presumably replaced the nearby South Shunters Cabin that was demolished in 1971.

Top Right : A view from the site of No 1 Yard towards the reception sidings. The South Shunters Cabin stood to the left of the buffer stops. The parapets of the adjacent under bridge are just visible. The air raid shelter to the right was one of the last buildings to remain standing.

Bottom Right : The underpass (Bridge No 3) by the South Shunters Cabin in the process of being filled in during January 1999.

Endings and Beginnings : The Authors perspective

When my parents moved to Mapperley in 1970, they bought a house overlooking the Trent Valley. From the back garden Colwick could be seen in the far distance. Looking through my father's binoculars, long rakes of old freight stock and coaches could be made out, lined up awaiting disposal. If you watched long enough you saw the odd train on the neighbouring Grantham line, and if you were really lucky, a train on the Colwick Estates Railway To a five year old this was fascinating, and I still remember the disappointment when the sidings were cleared the next year.

Later I was to become better acquainted with the site of Colwick sidings. A school friend had lived in one of the old railway houses in Traffic Terrace and shared an interest in trains. We spent many hours together exploring the wilderness that had once been occupied by a bustling loco shed and busy freight yard.

Above : No 1 Yard, close to the site of Carlton Fields. By 1983 little remained and the site was in the early stages of development, with sewer pipes poised for laying. The gutted office and platform were at the western end of the yard, at a location denoted on plans as being a Tranships Stage.

Right : Rectory Junction box, and the last remaining semaphore, seen in June 2005. Signal 74 controls the old yard entry line, now used as a cripple road for defective wagons. The appearance of the box has been changed by replacement windows and removal of the exterior catwalk.

By this time, aside from a few huts, most of the buildings had been levelled, although it was still possible to see where they had stood. A great deal of rubble remained. I clearly remember the part filled inspection pits, and clambering into the abandoned wet ash pits to explore. The most striking impression of the site was its enormous size. Mountains of broken brick and concrete, together with huge piles of ballast and an almost total lack of vegetation gave the western side of the site an appearance not unlike the surface of the moon, albeit punctuated by abandoned and broken railway equipment.

One could easily get lost wandering about these acres of undulating wilderness. There were few recognisable features and it might be necessary to clamber up a pile of rubble or the odd remaining signal post to get your bearings. Signal box locations were discernable in a couple of places, with rows of broken cast iron bellcrank and pulley bases bearing the initials 'LNER' still in place on the leading in timbers. Rows of derelict railway houses along the western boundary of the site displayed cast iron name plates like Locomotive Terrace and London and North Western Terrace, betraying their origins.

Occasionally interesting finds would turn up in the rubble. Anything with a railway company identity that was small enough to rescue went in the bicycle saddlebag for taking home, much to my parents despair. My prize find was a GNR wagon plate from a 10T open, discovered almost completely buried in the ash near to the site of the old shed.

destined presumably for the Colwick Industrial Estate. We never explored here since it was clearly still used, and we had no desire to get in trouble with the railway police.

Industrial estate workings could be observed from Private Road No 3. The Class 08 shunter used on the branch could be followed by bicycle as it trundled along the roadside between petrochemical plants collecting four-wheel tank wagons. The Colwick Estates Light Railway extended as far as Mile End Road, where the Sugar Beet factory had a rail connection. An antiquated rail mounted steam crane stood rusting in the yard accompanied by rotting timber-built wagons and a decrepit four wheel diesel shunter. All were painted in the same peeling blue livery of the British Sugar Corporation and looked to be long abandoned.

My interest in photography was just starting and to my regret, I took very few pictures at Colwick. I little realised that these shadows and reminders of what had been would soon be gone entirely.

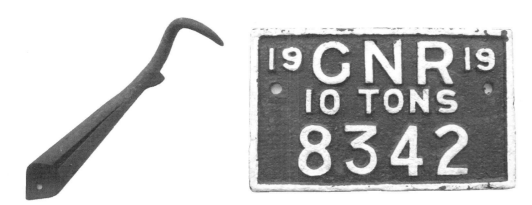

Two reminders of Colwick Yards. The head from a Shunters pole, used for uncoupling wagons, and a cast iron plate found in the vicinity of the GN depot. The plate is from a standard 5 plank 10 Ton open used by the Great Northern, and appropriately known as a "Colwick Wagon". Examples of "junk" rescued on foraging trips in the early 1980s.

The eastern side of the site was a featureless plain of scarified ballast that stretched away as far as the eye could see. Over towards the Grantham line, tracks were still there and occasionally groups of wagons were parked up,

Class 08 No 08858 was a regular performer on the Colwick Estates Light Railway. It is seen here propelling an air braked guards van across the Private Road No 3 crossing in May 1979. This particular trip had seen a short rake of 45 tonne tankers delivered to one of the Estate's petrochemical storage plants The indifferent photograph is a reflection of the lens quality on the Author's first camera; a Kodak Brownie 127.

4. The GNR "Back Line"

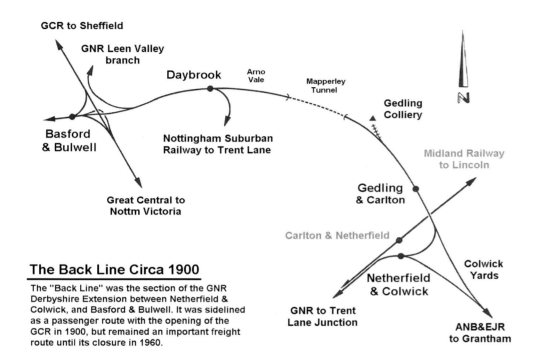

The Back Line Circa 1900

The "Back Line" was the section of the GNR Derbyshire Extension between Netherfield & Colwick, and Basford & Bulwell. It was sidelined as a passenger route with the opening of the GCR in 1900, but remained an important freight route until its closure in 1960.

A Description of the Route

The GNR Derbyshire Extension opened in 1875. It ran from a triangular junction with the Ambergate's Grantham line at Colwick, skirting north around Nottingham's outer suburbs of Gedling, Mapperley and Woodthorpe, before turning west and heading for Derby. The section between Colwick and Basford & Bulwell was known locally as the "Back Line". Built to substantial standards, this double line climbed away from Colwick at 1 in 100 for the first three miles, passing through the first station at Gedling on the way to the summit at Arno Vale. The route passed through the 1132 yd long Mapperley Tunnel along the way. Gedling Colliery was sunk to the east of here at the beginning of the Twentieth Century and as it developed; its rail connection would eventually contribute a significant amount of traffic to the line.

Once clear of the tunnel, the line crossed rolling open countryside as it headed towards Arno Vale. Passing loops were initially provided here, with a small signal cabin provided to control them. A short distance to the west the next station was

reached at Daybrook. A trailing junction was built to the east of here in 1889, connecting with the Nottingham Suburban Railway (see chapter 4).

A second junction to the west of Daybrook opened in 1881, when a new line pushed north along the Leen Valley to Bestwood, Hucknall and beyond, tapping lucrative coal traffic previously monopolised by the Midland Railway. A goods road and exchange sidings were provided west of Daybrook to cope with the extra traffic.

The third stop on the route was Basford & Bulwell. This busy station assumed greater importance when the GCR main line crossed the route nearby in 1899. Connections were provided between both lines in both directions, with carriage sidings constructed in the space between the two routes.

To the west of Basford and Bulwell Station the line crossed over the Midland Railway's Leen Valley branch, before pushing west towards Cinderhill, Kimberley and on into Derbyshire (see Volume 2).

Netherfield & Colwick marked the eastern end of the GNR Derbyshire extension; although a second east facing junction existed at Rectory. The station was not built until 3 years after the Derbyshire Extension opened. By 1958 the station buildings were in a dilapidated state, with large sections of the awnings missing. The buildings were demolished just two years after this photograph, to be replaced with a utilitarian flat roofed structure that owed much of its appearance to Portacabin design.

N(B)MRS /D R Morley

Traffic

The GNR selected a route for its new line around Nottingham's northern outskirts, in order to avoid dense urban areas, reduce construction time and minimise costs. This would also provide freight with a direct route from the Notts and Derbys coalfields to the expanding yards at Colwick.

The line crossed Netherfield Lane (now Victoria Road) just a few hundred yards from Colwick West Junction. The box controlling the crossing, and entry to the adjacent goods yard was built in 1875 and contained 13 levers. It is seen here towards the end of its life in March 1981. The line was just a colliery branch by this date, and the box only opened when the crossing gates required working.

Coal was the Derbyshire Extensions primary business. Pits along the network of connecting lines, together with those at Gedling and Cinderhill generated a huge volume of traffic. Most of this was routed through Colwick Yard. Empties for points north and west filed past Colwick North Junction at the start of their long climb towards Mapperley Tunnel, whilst loaded coal trains destined for Colwick from the Erewash and Leen valleys, Cinderhill and Gedling descended the 1 in 100 grade through Gedling Station towards the No 5 reception yard. Traffic was so great that Colwick sidings would evolve to become the largest facility of its kind in Europe.

The Derbyshire Extension did not however provide the most direct of routes for passengers travelling from Nottingham. Trains from London Road needed to travel three miles in the wrong direction before gaining the new line, and then head north for two more miles before finally turning west. City Councillors had long lobbied the Railway companies to build a new station in the heart of Nottingham, with direct routes to neighbouring towns. They would have to wait until 1901 to get their way.

With the opening of Nottingham Victoria Station, Derby trains were re-routed via the new joint line to Bagthorpe Junction, saving seven miles on the journey. This left the portion between Netherfield and Bagthorpe Junction with primarily freight workings, together with a few local passenger services. Opening of the new junctions at Bagthorpe and Trent Lane meant that GNR trains from Victoria destined for Basford & Bulwell could depart in both directions. Likewise trains on the Back line destined for Victoria travelled both east and west. This must have been a source of some confusion to travellers unfamiliar with the area.

The Stations

Stations along the line were generally constructed to variations of a standard design. This comprised a substantial two storey station house in local red brick on the main platform, with a range of single storey structures attached, containing waiting rooms, booking offices and toilet facilities. The facing platform generally had a hipped roof timber-built waiting room to a generic design used widely across the East Midlands.

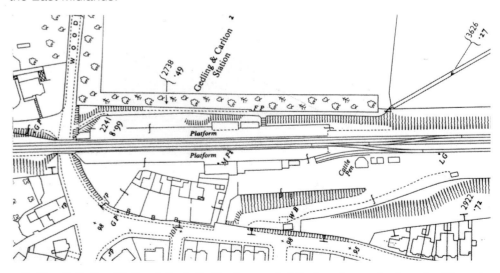

Gedling & Carlton Station (latterly Gedling) was set at the top of an embankment, with road access to the yard by means of a ramp. By the 1954 publication date of this 1:2500 Scale Ordnance Survey plan, residential development was already beginning to hem the site in.

Pictured here some 25 years after closure in 1985, the main station buildings at Gedling have found a new use. Converted into a youth centre, they retain much of their original appearance on the platform side. The windows have been changed, and several doorways blocked off, but the architectural style is still distinctively Great Northern. The other side of the building has fared less well, being partially obscured by a large and ill matching extension housing sporting facilities. Trains were still running to Gedling Colliery when this photograph was taken, and the track was in a reasonable state of maintenance. Today this view is completely obscured by trees, and little can be seen of the old station. The photograph above is a composite of five separate shots, since the ground levels and presence of trees would not permit a single photograph of the elevation.

The station at Basford & Bulwell (later renamed Basford North) differed from others on the line in being constructed from local Bulwell Stone and sporting some notably ornate chimney stacks. Train capacity was increased here by construction of a third platform face when the GCR arrived.

Yards with substantial goods facilities were provided at Daybrook and Basford & Bulwell, but facilities at Gedling were sparse, consisting of a single siding. The junction station at Netherfield and Colwick also had no yard, but facilities were provided between here and Gedling, alongside the locomotive depot at Colwick.

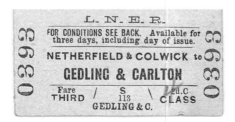

Above : LNER tickets for Back Line journeys were still being issued in the Fifties.

Class O1 No 63768 of Colwick Shed drifts through Gedling Station light engine on its way to Gedling Colliery early in 1957. The station was to close three years later.

C A Hill

Robinson O4/7 No 63891 is given a clear road through Gedling Station with an Up working destined for Colwick Yard. 18th February 1955.

N(B)MRS / D R Morley

This wintry scene was recorded at Gedling on Friday 18th February 1955. The yard here consisted of a single siding and loading dock. Full goods facilities were provided to the North of Netherfield & Colwick at Victoria Road.

N(B)MRS / D R Morley

Some Ongoing Maintenance Problems

Almost all of the structures on the Back Line appear to have suffered maintenance problems, and few escaped rebuilding or major repairs. Mining subsidence was a particular difficulty and this was identified as causing the collapse of a short section of Mapperley Tunnel in 1925.

The tunnel had a reputation for being wet. Several former loco men known to the Author have related instances of engines struggling to gain a footing as they climbed the 1 in 100 gradient through it. Saturation of clay reduces its shear strength, making it more susceptible to movement. A combination of poor drainage, clay soil and mining activity at nearby Gedling Colliery more or less assured problems with subsidence.

This was not the only difficulty however. Another factor appears to have been the quality of brick used by the original Contractors. Many smaller bridges on the line were constructed in a semi-porous red brick. It appears that poor drainage design and a lack of maintenance allowed moisture ingress into the masonry. The brickwork suffered badly under frost action, and there is evidence to suggest that spalling bricks were an ongoing problem. Inspection of the few sections of original structure that survive today reveals extensive repairs carried out progressively in a variety of materials over a protracted time period.

Lambley Lane (Bridge 17) was just one of many to be replaced on the line during LNER and BR ownership, owing to subsidence damage and deterioration of the brickwork. The Up line had been removed by the time this view was recorded in 1983, and a minewater pipeline constructed along the cess of the redundant side of the formation. This transported water from Gedling Colliery to a lagoon close to Rectory Junction.

A combination of deterioration and mining subsidence led to several bridges being replaced completely during LNER days, and further repairs were carried out after nationalisation. By the time the line closed, few of the original structures remained as built.

It was subsidence that finally finished the Back Line to through traffic. Mapperley Tunnel had long been known to have problems, and by the late Fifties movement of the lining at the eastern end had again become cause for concern. A temporary timber support was built into the crown of the east portal to buy time whilst schemes were considered to remedy the situation. Several options were considered, but the new London Midland Regional management deemed the most cost effective solution to be closure of the Back Line altogether, diverting all through traffic via Nottingham Victoria. The section closed to through traffic on 4th April 1960 (although anecdotal evidence suggests a few movements using the line after this). Passenger services were withdrawn from Gedling and Daybrook. Freight services were maintained, but with access taken from opposite ends of the line.

Class O4/7 No 63839 is just about to pass beneath Lambley Lane with a train of empties from Colwick Yard on Saturday 18th June 1955.

N(B)MRS / D R Morley

Class O4/4 No 63745 is seen near Lambley Lane as it climbs the incline towards Arno Vale Summit, on 18th June 1955. The Locomotive is one of Colwick's allocation and the train comprises loaded iron ore hoppers destined for Stanton Ironworks. After the closure of Mapperley tunnel, these workings were diverted via Weekday Cross Junction and the GCR.

N(B)MRS / D R Morley

O4/1 No 63684 drifts down the 1 in 100 past Gedling Colliery with a loaded coal train from off the Leen Valley. Gedling Colliery Signal Box is visible in the distance, together with a train waiting for a path out onto the main line.

N(B)MRS / D R Morley

The same view some thirty years later shows a much changed scene, with the Up line gone and the distant slag heaps graded into much gentler mounds, a legacy of the Aberfan disaster.

The line after Closure

Closure of the Derbyshire Extension was not quite the end of the story. A little over two miles of the line at its eastern end continued to be used by trains serving Gedling Colliery for another 30 years. The track was singled in 1966, and from 1968 the line was operated by token from Netherfield Junction signal box.

A surprising amount of period infrastructure lasted on the line until comparatively recently. The 1878 Netherfield Lane signal box remained in use until 1982 to work the adjacent level crossing. The hand-wheel operated gates continued to carry oil lamps and LNER upper quadrant signals on lattice posts protected the crossing in each direction, albeit now worked from Netherfield Junction. The adjacent goods depot buildings survived intact, used by a road haulier, and telegraph poles were still in place on the down side. Old cast iron and enamelled signs lent additional atmosphere. The gates, cabin, signals and telegraph poles were all removed in 1982, and an unmanned open crossing installed.

Within weeks of the new crossing being commissioned a City Transport bus was hit by a coal train and dragged along the line. Miraculously nobody was killed. The train was able to pull up within fifty yards owing to its low speed and unloaded condition. Following this, half-barriers were installed.

Class 20 20090 of Toton Depot double heads an unidentified engine of the same class on a loaded HAA working past the closed station at Gedling in early 1985. The two pipes in the foreground carry waste water from Gedling Colliery.

Further up the line at Colwick North Junction, the brick base to the signal box was left in-situ after removal of the superstructure in 1971. Today it still perches on the side of the embankment behind Chandos Street allotments, together with two of the telegraph poles that once carried wires to the box.

A little to the north of here the main block of buildings at Gedling Station escaped demolition, finding new use as a local youth centre. Residential development has encroached on the down side goods yard, whilst the site of the up side platform are now covered by trees and brambles.

Colliery Workings

Trains in the Sixties were usually worked by Colwick based Type 2 Diesel-Electrics (Class 20s) and comprised initially of 16T mineral wagons, or LNER derived 21T and 24T hoppers with a single 20T brake. Workings were initially routed via Carlton Fields into Colwick Sidings until closure of the yards, after which trains were routed to Toton via Netherfield Junction. In the 1970s 16T wagons were phased out. The aging hopper wagons continued for more than a decade and the Gedling trip became the last diagram in the country for these vintage wagons. They were withdrawn in the late eighties when loading plant at Gedling Colliery was adapted to handle newer wagon designs. Final workings utilised HAA stock, with motive power including Class 56s and 58s.

A pair of Class 20s come off the Gedling Colliery line at Netherfield & Colwick in 1983. The wagons behind are a mixture of 21T and 24T vehicles dating back to the steam era.

The last chapter was written in February 2002, when a railtour visited the line. Hauled by a pair of preserved Class 33s, and banked by a Class 56, the stock comprised Mark 1 and 2 carriages. Running late and arriving as dusk fell the working came as a surprise to many local residents, the line not having seen a passenger train in four decades.

A pair of Sulzer Class 33 locomotives head up the curve on the western leg of the Colwick triangle with a railtour in early 2002. The train has just passed beneath the A612. The bare land to the right was once occupied by engine roads to the north of Colwick Shed. Today this area has disappeared beneath new road development.

Gedling Colliery in later years

Even in latter years Gedling Colliery still retained many links with the past. A selection of interesting internal user stock could often be found parked up in the further reaches of the yard. Ancient timber bodied private owner wagons with wooden solebars were in use right up to the end of the Colliery's existence. Some wagons parked up at Mapperley Landsale Wharf even had private owner names including "Digby" and "Gedling" showing from beneath peeling black NCB paint.

Steam haulage had finished at the colliery in the early Seventies, but the four wheel diesel hydraulics that replaced the Barclay saddle tanks pottered about the site until the end. Some track in the complex had not been relayed since pre-grouping days, and as late as 1990 the headshunt at the junction with the main line was still equipped with GN bullhead chairs bearing 1890s dates.

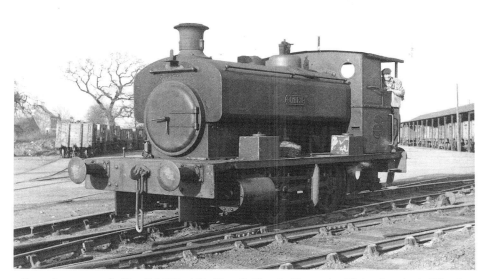

Two views recorded by C A Hill at Gedling Colliery's Mapperley Plains Landsale Wharf .

Top ; 1923 built Barclay saddle tank "Queen" No 1784 is seen in 1960 .

Below : Barclay six-coupled tank of 1903 (Works No 1000) "Catherine" photographed in 1956.

Barclay were not the only manufacturer represented at Gedling. Peckett 0-6-0 ST "Audrey" , built in 1911, is seen here in the Colliery yard in 1961.

C A Hill

The final shunting engines employed at Gedling were Thomas Hill diesel-hydraulics. One of these was caught by the Author's camera at Mapperley Landsale Wharf in 1982.

The closure of the colliery in 1991 led to the line being mothballed. It was briefly reopened in 1999 whilst tailings were recovered from the tip, but this finished within a year, after the operation was abandoned as uneconomic. Today the disused route is heavily overgrown, but safeguarded for potential reuse as a heavy rail commuter link into Nottingham from a projected park and ride facility on the former colliery site.

Removal of a Railway

To the west of Gedling Colliery the line was lifted after closure, and redevelopment quickly claimed much of the formation. A few traces have survived, but these are well hidden. Mapperley tunnel approach cuttings remain, although each are in private land and inaccessible. The west portal was filled over long ago, but the eastern end is still open at the time of writing. The line was closed due to instability of this tunnel, and temporary timber shoring put in by BR during the fifties continues to support the cracked brickwork at the portal. The bore is open as far as the surface vent at "Pepperpots" scout hut on Plains Road, but backfilled beyond this.

Above : Mapperley Tunnel is seen here in 1989. Deterioration of the tunnel portal is evident, and the copings on the parapet have been pushed off.

Below : By 1982 the crumbling remains of Mapperley Tunnel were overgrown and forgotten by all but local children and railway historians.

Bridge No 21 was rebuilt by the LNER after the original structure was damaged by subsidence. After abandonment, the cutting was filled. This subsequently settled, leaving the upper section of the structure visible. It is seen in 1988. Today it is completely obscured by trees.

A short section of trackbed alongside Arnot Hill Park, to the east of the Suburban Railway junction has found a new use as a walkway, but Thackerays Lane Bridge (No 24) has been replaced with a modern concrete underpass. The bridge across Mansfield Road was removed during the early Seventies. No trace remains of Daybrook Station or the yard beyond it, and the site is now occupied by a retail park development.

Further west, City Council reclamation projects have now removed almost every trace of the route. Housing estates or landscaped school grounds occupy sites once used by exchange traffic for the Leen Valley branch and coal trains destined for Colwick and the eastern counties. Park Lane overbridge to the east of Basford & Bulwell is the only surviving structure inside the city limits, although the deck was replaced in the lines final years with a modern concrete design, and the refuges in the abutments have been bricked up.

Basford & Bulwell Station, like Daybrook disappeared not long after closure, and today the site is occupied by commercial development, with no trace of the railway or its earthworks remaining.

Above : The soffit of the tunnel is showed here at the south ventilation shaft. The protective grill is just visible at the top of the shaft.

Below : An unusual relic abandoned in the cess deep inside the tunnel is this locomotive buffer. A Colwick Fireman that the Author knew related a story of one of their eight-coupled freight locos losing a buffer on this part of line in the late Fifties. Could this be that buffer?

In happier times Ivatt J1 No 65007 of Colwick Shed is seen climbing away from the west side of Mapperley Tunnel. This photograph taken in early 1951 records a Nottingham Victoria to Basford stopping train. The open rolling countryside in this view has now been completely swamped by housing development and little trace of the Derbyshire Extension remains.

C A Hill

With regulator open 8F No 48090 climbs away from Mapperley Tunnel with a Colwick to Ellesmere Port tanker train in 1958. Transfer of the line to London Midland Region saw an increase in the appearance of LMS locomotive types.

C A Hill

Gresley K3 No 61914 heads east with an East Coast excursion in the summer of 1957. Bridge 24 is visible in the background and the train is about to reach the summit at Arno Vale, before dropping down the long 1 in 100 through Gedling to Colwick.

C A Hill

Class O4/1 No 63829 climbs tender first towards Arno Vale, and east to Colwick Yard. This loaded coal train from the Leen Valley was recorded early in 1957.

C A Hill

Austerity No 90624 approaches Hallam Lane (now Thackerays Lane) bridge (No 24) with an Up freight destined for Colwick in 1957. The bridge was demolished a short while after closure and replaced with a concrete underpass.

C A Hill

Colwick J6 No 64257 is seen working tender first with a Nottingham Victoria train in 1957. This locomotive was equipped with a screen on the cab, to give the crew some weather protection when working tender first.

C A Hill

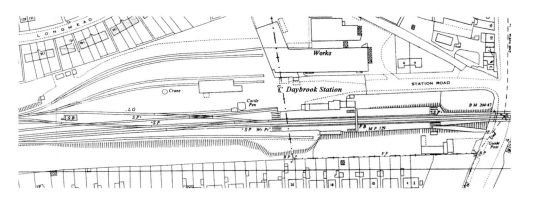

Daybrook Station's full title was Daybrook for Arnold & Bestwood. The 1954 1:2500 Ordnance Survey shows the station layout towards the end of its existence. It closed to passengers on 4th April 1960 and to goods four years later.

Local Photographer Tony Hill lived a short distance from Daybrook Station and he took many photographs in the final years of the lines operation. Daybrook Station is shown to good effect in this 1955 view, looking west.

C A Hill

By 1966 Daybrook Station was in a sorry state. The last tracks had been lifted two years earlier, and the footbridge and signal box had been demolished. The Station building was derelict and the end was clearly near.

C A Hill

Edwards Lane bridge (No 29) underwent significant alteration during its life. The original single span had a second single track span added on the north side when the Leen Valley Line opened in 1880. The whole structure was then widened in the 1930s, and its parapets replaced to accommodate improvements to Edwards Lane. The bridge, shown here circa 1980 was in filled in about 1990, and today no trace remains.

Nottingham City Council

Park Lane Bridge (No 35) was rebuilt very late in the life of the line. The original wrought iron structure had badly corroded by the 1960s, and incredibly it was replaced by BR in 1965 with the reinforced concrete deck seen here.

Nottingham City Council

Hucknall Road bridge (32) was widened at the same time as Edwards Lane. It underwent extensive repairs to the frost damaged masonry, and the entire arch face was cement rendered. The cutting beyond was filled during the Seventies, and the bridge, pictured here in 1983 was infilled by the City Council during 1999.

The deck of the structure was too shallow to accommodate water and gas mains, which were carried on the outside. Individual baffles were attached to each pipe to deflect the exhaust blast of passing locomotives. Refuges were incorporated into the abutments, but these have now been bricked up to deter anti-social behaviour.

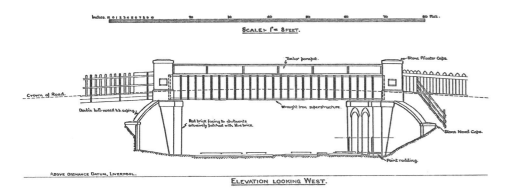

The original deck of Bridge 35 is seen in this 1943 elevation produced by the LNER Engineer's Office. It reveals some surprising detail, such as the timber parapets. At this time concrete tank traps were situated in the footway and carriageway on the south approach to the bridge.

Nottingham City Council

A red, cream and blue striped third class workman's weekly ticket issued in April 1904 for travel between Basford & Bulwell, and Daybrook stations.

Ian Askew Collection

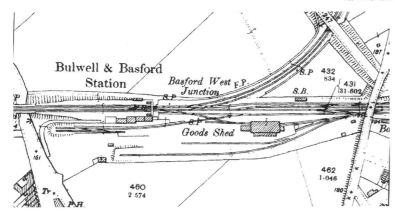

Basford & Bulwell Station is shown as it appeared on the 1902 County Series Ordnance Survey. It was renamed Basford North in 1953, and closed to passengers in 1964.

Brooklyn Road joins Park Lane close to the site of Basford West Junction. Here a two track chord connected with the Great Central. Bridge No 2 on this short section was a standard GC design, comprising blue brick abutments and wing walls, with a steel deck. It was completed in 1898, and in filled by the City Council in 1988.

The Great Central was accessed to the south by two separate chords from Basford East Junction, to the east of Park Lane. The Down line crossed over Arnold Road, whilst the Up line, having burrowed beneath the GC, then passed beneath Arnold Road. This latter structure was blue brick with a steel superstructure. The tunnel and cuttings were filled almost as soon as the rails were lifted. Arnold Road Bridge was to be excavated in 1980 however, to provide a haul route for Contractors wagons engaged in the reclamation of the GC alignment. The bridge was in surprisingly good order considering it had been buried for more than a decade. A year later it disappeared again when the cutting was refilled.

Nottingham City Council

5. The Nottingham Suburban Railway

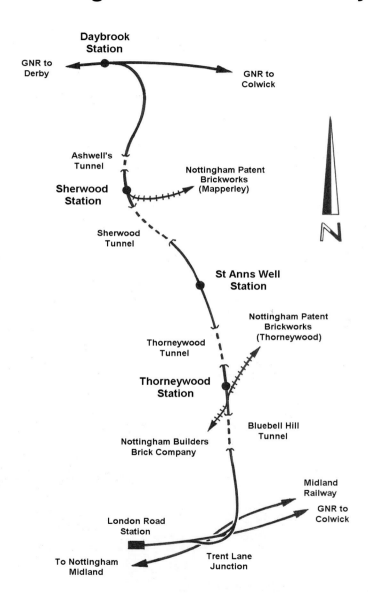

Above : Route plan of the Nottingham Suburban Railway as it was at the time of opening in 1889. Thirteen years later the construction of the GCR and Nottingham Victoria Station led to a further connection at Trent Lane, leading to Weekday Cross.

Background

The Nottingham Suburban Railway Act of 25th June 1886 granted Parliamentary powers for the construction of a new independent railway line. It would run north from a junction with the Great Northern Railway at Trent Lane in Sneinton, to a new junction at Daybrook on the GN's Derbyshire Extension. The line measured three miles, five furlongs and two chains in length. Construction began in June 1887 with the sinking of a shaft for the excavation of Sherwood Tunnel. The line took two years to complete, opening in August 1889.

Nominally an independent concern backed by local businessmen and brick manufacturers, the railway was operated by the Great Northern under agreement from opening, and the line was subsequently leased to them.

Sherwood Tunnel was 442 yards long, with a reverse curve to its alignment, meaning that it was only possible to see each end from a short section in the middle. The northern end of this tunnel was constructed slightly longer than originally planned, to avoid disturbing the local farmer's stackyard. Work began on the line here on June 13th 1887, with the sinking of a 90 foot deep shaft from land owned by the Nottingham Patent Brick Company, adjacent to Woodborough Road.

C A Hill

Civil Engineering

The line required some substantial feats of engineering in order to traverse the undulating eastern side of the City. The nature of the terrain was such that practically all of the line was built in cutting or on embankment. The line climbed 200 feet from Trent Lane to the summit at Sherwood, in a series of stiff gradients to a maximum of 1 in 50. Four tunnels were needed, together with a total of fourteen bridges. A wrought iron bowstring flyover constructed by the Butterley Engineering Company carried the southbound line across the GNR in two spans of 75 and 125 feet at Trent Lane Junction, and a viaduct crossed The Wells Road (demolishing the medieval St Ann's Well in the process). Massive retaining walls enclosed the station site at Thorneywood, similar to those that would be required at Victoria more than a decade later.

Situated 1 mile and 15 chains from Trent Lane, Bridge No 7 was an expensive and difficult structure to build. It had a skew angle of around 45 degrees, and was constructed with the deck inclined at 1 in 20 to match the fall of the road. The 15 cross beams were shaped to match the profile of the road and the fixed headroom of 14' 6". The railway was laid to a climbing gradient of 1 in 48 at this point. After nearly thirty years of dereliction, it was infilled in 1983 to accommodate a road improvement.

Structures on the line were solidly constructed and faced with engineering blue bricks, contrasting with the poorer quality materials that appear to have typified earlier GNR built lines in the area. The choice of more expensive materials reflected in the durability of the structures. The masonry elements appear to have required little or no maintenance, demonstrated in the fact that the bridges surviving today are still in excellent condition.

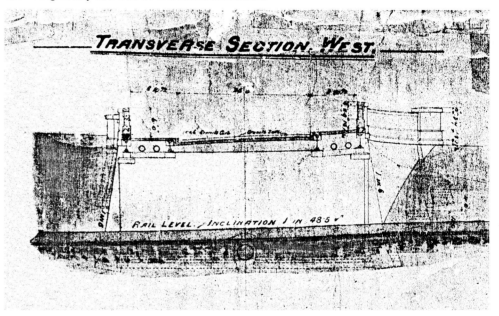

Extract from the original, if somewhat damaged 1885 design drawings for Bridge No 7. It shows the western abutment, the single curving wing wall adjacent to the station approaches and the unusual profile of the wrought iron cross-beams. Some 70 Tons of wrought iron was incorporated into the deck of this bridge.

Stations were provided at Thorneywood, St Ann's Well and Sherwood. Facilities were modest but well built, with station buildings constructed in red brick made locally by the Nottingham Patent Brick Company, who had been a key sponsor of the line's construction. Goods facilities were provided at each station, which included a small single storey shed, a hand worked crane and a weighbridge.

Mapperley and Thorneywood supported a thriving brick-making industry which stretched back to the early part of the 18th Century. The Nottingham Patent Brick Company supplied their products nationally and elements of St Pancras Station were reputably built using bricks made at Mapperley. The landscape in this area eventually came to be dominated by marl pits, kiln chimneys and tramways. Engine worked rope-hauled inclines connected brickworks with exchange sidings at Sherwood and Thorneywood stations. The Mapperley incline passed beneath a finely proportioned brick arch at its lower end, carrying Sherwood Rise, which provided road access to the Patent Company's brick yards. The incline at the same company's works at Thorneywood was more unusual in that it ran underground along the line of Burgass Road, emerging through a portal in the station retaining wall just to the north of Carlton Road bridge. To the south of the bridge lay a further brickworks siding, serving the rival Builders Brick Company. This company extracted clay to the west of, and directly above Bluebell Hill Tunnel.

Traffic

When the Suburban Line was planned, the Shareholders held high hopes for it. The GNR would divert its Derby Friargate to London Road services via the new line, to bypass the run out to Colwick and up the "Back Line". The MS&LR (latterly the GCR) could run its own trains from Sheffield into Nottingham on the line, via its extension to Annesley, and the GNR Leen Valley route. Even traffic from the L&NWR was envisaged. The Nottingham Corporation was also keen to support the venture, and had visions of new suburbs springing up alongside the railway.

 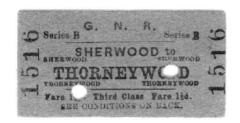

Tickets from the Nottingham Suburban Railway are something of a rarity. Both of these are GNR blue third class tickets dating from April 1904. The left hand ticket was for a journey involving a change of trains at Daybrook.

Ian Askew Collection

The line opened in 1889, and controversy marked the opening day, when, as a result of a financial dispute, the Contractor attempted to stop the first train entering the line. Unfortunately the line was only to have a very short useful life, and it never generated the traffic or the dividends that the Shareholders had anticipated. The GNR failed to divert the amount of traffic to it that the Company had hoped for, and construction of the Great Central's London Extension in 1899 effectively bypassed it. To make matters worse, from 1901, expanding Corporation tram services took away virtually all of the remaining passengers. With ticket revenues almost non-existent the stations were closed to passengers in 1916, ostensibly as a wartime economy measure. They never reopened and the line, with its reduced status was singled in 1930.

The brickyards provided just enough traffic to keep the line open as a freight route, and occasional diversions would use the line if engineering work was being undertaken on the Back Line.

The busiest period of operation in the lines history came in 1925, when a section of Mapperley Tunnel collapsed. All Back Line workings, including trains for the Leen Valley route and freight traffic destined for Colwick, were diverted along the Suburban line whilst the tunnel was repaired.

The foot of the brickworks incline at Sherwood is seen here. The bridge carrying what is now Sherwood Vale was classified as Bridge No 12, by the GNR, although it actually spanned private tracks. Judging by the appearance of the incline, traffic had presumably ceased by the time this 1952 view was recorded. The GNR bridge Number plate is visible on the left abutment.

C A Hill

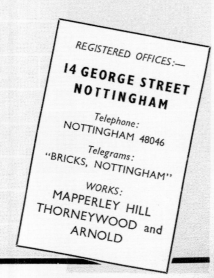

THE NOTTINGHAM PATENT BRICK COMPANY LTD

Manufacturers of
WIRE-CUT COMMON
WIRE-CUT COMMON SELECTED

THE LARGEST MANUFACTURERS OF BRICKS IN THE DISTRICT!

Sole Manufacturers of

- **NUTEC FACINGS**
- **HANTEC FACINGS**
- **RUFTEC FACINGS**
- **SMUTEC FACINGS**

(B.T.M. Reg. 536873, 608752, 608753, 608754)

These FACING BRICKS are manufactured in a large variety of colours, and have been used in many schools and public buildings in various parts of the country

- Inspection invited of **FACING BRICKS** in bulk at the Works and Buildings erected therewith

REGISTERED OFFICES:—
14 GEORGE STREET NOTTINGHAM

Telephone:
NOTTINGHAM 48046

Telegrams:
"BRICKS, NOTTINGHAM"

WORKS:
MAPPERLEY HILL
THORNEYWOOD and
ARNOLD

132

The Nottingham Patent Brick Company still operated out of its sites at Mapperley and Thorneywood in the late 1950s, as this advertisement demonstrates. By this time the railway had closed, and the company's products were being moved by road.

Author's Collection

In 1928 the stations at Sherwood and Thorneywood received a fresh coat of paint and were tidied up for a special event. King George V and Queen Mary visited Woodthorpe Park, and these stations were temporarily reopened to serve special trains laid on to transport schoolchildren to the park for the event. After the excitement of the day, the station doors closed once more and the line settled back into obscurity.

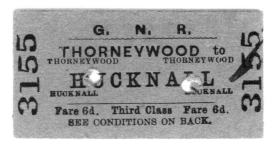

A blue GNR third class ticket from Ian Askew's extensive collection. It dates from 29th April 1904 and the train would have originated from the recently opened Nottingham Victoria.

Ian Askew Collection

Through working finished when the embankment to the north of Trent Lane Junction was hit by German bombs in 1941. The damaged was not repaired, and the remaining section from Daybrook to Thorneywood operated until 1954 as a long siding from Daybrook Junction (see Appendix 3). The southern stub across the flyover at Trent Lane was used for wagon storage.

The Nottingham Patent Brick Company continued provided dwindling traffic into the 1950s, but the Builders Brick Company site closed around the time of the Second World War. The site became an oil storage depot, and was rail served via the old brickworks access for a while.

The last passenger train to visit the Nottingham Suburban line was an RCTS Railtour hauled by C12 No 67386 in April 1951. Although the occasion is well documented, the days events (according to a Colwick fireman who worked this trip) may have been a little different to the version officially recorded.

The locomotive selected for the working was over 50 years old, and C12s were not renowned for their tractive abilities, even when new. The weight of the enthusiast's special combined with the stiff climb north from Thoneywood was clearly going to be a problem. The solution lay in banking the train with a J52 that Colwick had acquired from Whissendine. This informal "permissive working" would have been contrary to the operational rules for the line (one engine in steam unless coupled in multiple). The second engine therefore needed to stay hidden. To achieve this, the J52 was positioned out of site in Bluebell Hill tunnel, having previously worked a freight trip down to the yard at Thorneywood.

The special duly arrived at Thorneywood, where it was due to reverse. After the C12 had run around its train and the enthusiasts returned to their seats, the J52 drew forward and buffered up to the rear coach and the train departed north with the saddle tank assisting.

Thus the return trip of the last passenger train on the line was allegedly powered by two locomotives rather than one. The cover-up appears to have worked, because no photographs appear to have been taken of the J52 and details of this incident have never been published. But then of course it could all have been a tall tale from an old railwayman.

Freight continued for a further three years, finishing altogether early in 1954. The very last workings over the line were demolition and track recovery trains, handled by J6 and J52 locomotives working out of Colwick. By the end of 1954 their work was largely complete and apart from a few hundred yards of track at the Daybrook end, and the Up stub at Trent Lane Junction, the formation was stripped of its tracks.

Demolition

The wrought iron structures on the line were the first to be recovered, with the high price of scrap providing an incentive for early removal. The spans over the Midland and GN lines at Trent Lane were taken down by BR in 1954. Removal of the Warren Truss girder span across the Midland (Bridge No 1) created considerable excitement, when it was accidentally dropped on to the lines beneath. Nobody was injured, and damage to the tracks was not extensive. There was some delay to the reopening of the Midland line however, with services thrown into disruption (see Appendix 4).

Thorneywood Station is seen through the span of Bridge No 7 beneath Carlton Road in July 1955. The bridge still carries its GNR number plate, and the platforms and footbridge of the station are visible in the distance. The site was cleared four years later and a depot built for what was then the GPO's Telephone Branch.

N(B)MRS / D R Morley

Ownership of the remaining route passed to the City Council, and the span crossing The Wells Road was removed at about the same time. The brick approach spans to this were demolished in the early 1960s and the rubble was reputedly used to fill Thorneywood Tunnel. The track bed was progressively redeveloped through the 1960s and 1970s and little remains today. Sherwood Tunnel was filled in about 1970, and Ashwells Tunnel in the grounds of Woodthorpe Park was filled towards the end of that decade. Bluebell Hill Tunnel still exists as a shooting range with the north portal partially filled and bricked up, and the south portal completely buried. Bridges survive at Trent Lane, Sherwood Vale and Woodthorpe Drive, but the remainder are long gone, together with most of the alignment. The station houses at Thorneywood and St Ann's survive in private ownership.

Bridge 11 carried Sherwood Rise over the main tracks of the suburban line. It was positioned at the south end of the station platforms. The station was demolished progressively through the late fifties, and garages serving the block of flats in the background were built on the site in the 1960s. These have in turn been demolished and the site is now occupied by sheltered housing. This view was recorded in 1980.

In the line of fire. Bluebell Hill tunnel is the only one on the line to escape filling. It has found use as a shooting range, and was photographed in 1992.

Light Rail Revival?

During the late 1980s, Nottinghamshire County Council undertook a study into re-establishing the southern portion of the route to Thorneywood, as a possible light rail scheme. Drawings showing preliminary layouts for cuttings, embankments and structures were prepared and cost estimates drawn up. The proposal was eventually dropped, with the light rail project developing to the west side of the City instead. If the Suburban Railway had been selected then it would have been ironic indeed that it be reopened for use by trams, when they were responsible for closing it to passengers so long before.

Now you see it, now you don't.

In 1999 the British Telecom Marmion Road Depot was demolished, revealing the site of Thorneywood Station. The retaining walls, steel footbridge and brickworks tunnel portal were clearly visible for the first time in nearly forty years, together with the crown of Thorneywood Tunnel, where the infill had settled.

The formation of the line is seen here looking north in July 1955. The parapets of Sneinton Dale over bridge are visible, and in the background is Bluebell Hill Tunnel. It is already 13 years since through trains finished, and nature has started to reclaim the line.

N(B)MRS / D R Morley

The site of Thorneywood Station is seen here in 1999, immediately after clearance of the BT depot. The site was filled shortly afterwards with excavated material and demolition spoil from the Nottingham Ice Centre development. Once filled to ground level, the footbridge was removed and sheltered housing built over the site of the railway. The site of the tunnel to the Nottingham Patent Brick Company's yard was just behind the skip on the right of the picture.

The Thorneywood brickyard tunnel was opened by City Council Engineers in 1999, having been sealed for many years. After inspection, it was bricked back up and buried.

Nottingham City Coucil

The brickyard incline tunnel at Thorneywood was constructed with side refuges, in order that personnel on the line could avoid the path of rope hauled wagons.

Nottingham City Council

City Council Engineers took the opportunity to reopen the brickyard incline tunnel for inspection (it runs beneath a public highway, and a sewer has been laid along the centre of it). Nothing remained of the inclined plane, but the tunnel itself proved to be in surprisingly good condition. After being recorded, the end was re-sealed, and the cutting area in filled with rubble from the Nottingham Ice Arena development. With the site filled to surrounding ground level, the footbridge was then demolished. Sheltered housing now occupies the site and today there is little evidence to show that the railway ever existed.

The Tony Hill Collection

Local railway photographer Tony Hill lived close to the Suburban Railway at Woodthorpe. He had a great interest in the line, and after it closed he recorded the demise of the route in considerable detail. He, together with fellow enthusiast Joe Laidlow compiled and maintained a unique archive of photos and cuttings showing bridges, tunnels and buildings that have long since vanished. Sadly both have now passed on, and the Author is indebted to their friend John Bull, who kindly allowed access to this remarkable collection.

The following seven pages of photographs are believed to have been taken by Tony between 1955 and 1975. They follow the line from Trent Lane to Daybrook and show views that without exception, have changed beyond recognition.

Trent Lane Junction is shown in this group of views.

Above. By 1967 the trussed girder of Bridge No 1 had been removed, revealing this distant shot of the signal box, and part of the brick arch across Trent Lane.

Top Right: This 1957 view shows the abutment of Bridge No 1, viewed from over the parapet, immediately in front of Trent Lane Junction signal box. The Midland Railway crossing hut is visible on Trent Lane, together with one of the crossing gates.

Bottom Right: The Down Line rose at a gradient of 1 in 49 from the GNR tracks at Trent Lane. The bridge across the Midland Railway had just been removed in this 1957 view. The equipment stacked in the background is shoring used by the Contractor during demolition work.

Above : The junction at Trent Lane had changed dramatically by 1975. The GNR line to Colwick was now a single headshunt and the abandoned Suburban route was becoming overgrown.

Below : The abutment of Bridge No 3 across the Midland is seen here in 1957, just after removal of the steel deck. The split level of the bearing shelves is apparent in this view.

Above ; Bridge No 4 crossing Colwick Road was a conventional blue brick arch with generous headroom. In 1956 trolley buses still used Colwick Road, as can be seen by the wires.

Below : Bridge No 6 was a three span skew brick structure spanning Sneinton Dale. Photographed here in 1955, it was destroyed by explosives during the 1960s.

Above : Bluebell Hill Tunnel is seen in 1957. The formation is already strewn with rubbish and no trace remains of the industrial spur that once ran away to the right.

Below : Bridge No 7 carried Carlton Road across the line. The platform remains are visible in this view recorded in the same year.

Above : In 1955 the goods shed was the last rail level building remaining in place at Thorneywood Station. Thorneywood Tunnel can be seen in the background.

Below : The tunnel leading to the Nottingham Patent Brickworks was also visible in 1955, and would remain so until it was bricked up in about 1960.

Above : The Wells Road bridge seen in 1955 after removal of the main span. The 128 Ton deck had been manufactured by Messers Eastwood, Swingler & Co of Derby.

Below : The goods shed at St Anns Well was in a poor state of repair by 1956, It seems to have had been used by a haulier briefly, and the overgrown yard was littered with dumped vehicles.

Above : St Anns Well Station House survived the demolition of the station and is seen from the yard in 1955. It was still unoccupied in 1965, but today survives as apartments.

Below : In March 1967 the site of St Anns Well Station was being cleared for the construction of flats. Bentleys Bridge to the north was still intact at this time.

Above ; Sherwood Tunnel was the longest tunnel on the line at 442 yards. It is seen here in 1957. The tracks have been gone 3 years and the alignment is becoming quite overgrown.

Below: A general view of the remains of Sherwood Station in 1957. Bridge No 11 is still in good order and the platforms are clearly visible.

The Station House at Sherwood was very similar to those at Thorneywood and St Anns. It was the only one not to survive, being demolished shortly after this 1966 view.

Below : The Porter's Room on the Down platform at Sherwood surprisingly escaped the general demolition of the station and is seen here in 1955.

Above : Looking from Bridge No 11 towards Ashwells Tunnel in 1955. It seems barely credible that tracks had been here twelve months before. The signal box had burned down in 1953.

Below : Ashwells Tunnel is seen from the South in 1957. It remained a feature of Woodthorpe Park until it was filled in during the late 1970s.

Above : Looking up the brickworks incline through the arch of Bridge No 12 at Sherwood in 1955. Odd sleepers remain in situ, and as late as 1990, a few decaying sleepers were still in place near the foot of the incline. Today, aside from the bridge there is little to show that the incline ever existed and residential development has obliterated its route.

Above : Woodthorpe Drive (formerly Scout Lane) crossed the railway on a single span iron bridge In 1955 the route was still intact. Today gardens encroach over this section of line.

Below : The route of the Nottingham Suburban Railway is seen here stretching south from Thackerays Lane through suburbs it helped create, towards Woodthorpe Park.

Above : Thackerays Lane Bridge is seen in 1955. The structure was demolished in 1973 to accommodate a road improvement and housing development.

Below : End of the line. Daybrook junction is seen in 1955, with the single line connection still in situ, together with a short section of track and the protecting somersault signal.

6. The Great Central Railway

6.1 Nottingham Victoria Described

The London Extension of the Great Central Railway was the last main line to be built in the classic era of railway construction. Built between 1896 and 1899, it commenced at the south end of the company's existing Sheffield to Annesley line and passed through the heart of the East Midlands, on its way to London, and the new terminus station at Marylebone.

When the Great Central came to Nottingham, it cut ruthlessly through the heart of the old city. A vast area of decrepit slums, the Nottingham Workhouse and several taverns of ill repute were cleared away to make space for the new station, which was to be the most lavish and ornate in the region.

The lines were to be built some forty feet below street level, with the entire station enclosed in a brick lined cutting, and roofed over by a three span glass and steel train shed, supported by ornamented cast iron piers and the masonry of the two storey platform buildings. The plan layout was based around two very long island platforms, each over 1200 feet in length. At both ends of each island were 400 foot long bay platforms for local traffic. Beyond the train shed, the platforms were sheltered by awnings that stretched for a further 220 feet. Loco servicing facilities were provided at the departure end of the station in each direction, and these included two fifty foot turntables, coal stages and water cranes.

At platform level, passenger accommodation consisted of two large blocks of buildings on each island, finished in a buff glazed brick, and equipped with generously appointed waiting and refreshment rooms. At first floor level office accommodation was provided.

Two lattice steel footbridges crossed the site, one of which connected through to Glasshouse Street on the east side, the other of which allowed for distribution of passengers purely within the station. Two steel road bridges also crossed the site. Union Road Bridge was the larger, being some 280 feet in length, in five spans, with its corrugated steel deck being carried by steel cross girders. Parliament Street Bridge was also built of steel, with a trapezoidal deck spanning between 130 feet and 76 feet, as it crossed the converging lines at the south end of the site. This bridge incorporated small service tunnels beneath the footpaths, and had its steel parapets disguised with a red brick curtain wall in the road side. An access was built through the north parapet, with a distribution bridge and steps providing public access to the southern extremity of the two main island platforms.

The main booking hall and station entrance was located on Milton Street, and very imposing. Built in a Renaissance style to the design of A E Lambert, they featured an offset clock tower finished in red brick, with a copper clad cupola.

Above : Nottingham Victoria Station and its forecourt are seen here from the roof level of Trinity Square Car Park on 8th July 1967. The station would be swept away just a few months later, with only the clock tower remaining. Today, not only has the station gone, but also the car park from where this view was taken.

Ronald Askew

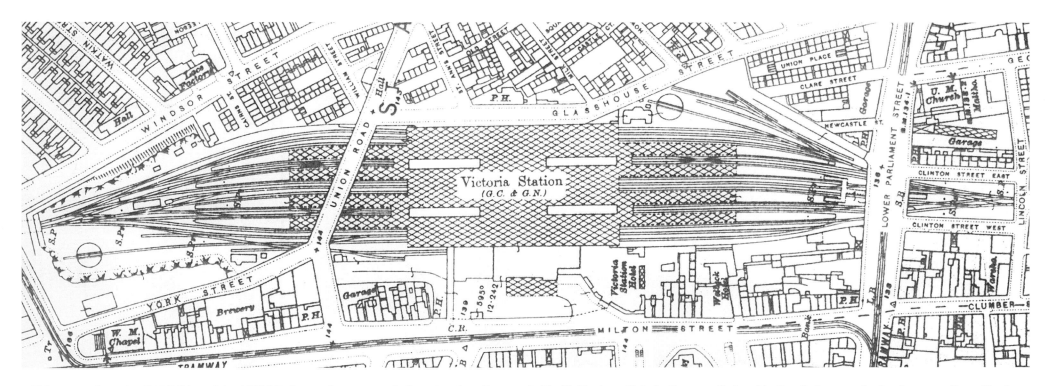

This extract from the 1915 Edition of the 1/2500 Ordnance Survey reveals the extensive site occupied by Nottingham Victoria. It was well placed in the city to serve the local community, unlike the more peripheral Midland Station. The bays and loco servicing facilities are clearly shown, together with the steel bridges that spanned the site, carrying Union Road and Parliament Street.. Detail beneath the overall roof is not recorded, but there were two further steel footbridges that crossed the site, one of which carried a public right of way through to Glasshouse Street. The cutting to the south of Parliament Street was hidden from public view by a high brick parapet wall and advertising hoardings.

Above : Three tickets from Nottingham Victoria in the British Railways period. The journey to Grantham was made on the 29th January 1960, and the fare had increased by sixpence since the ticket had been printed, judging by the handwritten price. The Journey from Netherfield and Colwick was made on the 7th February 1955, and was a half fare. The blue platform ticket on the right dates from roughly the same period, and would be familiar to any train spotter of the period.

Authors Collection

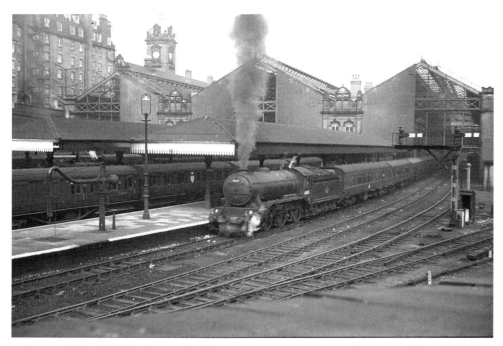

Gresley K3 No 61835 faces south with an express passenger working comprising BR Mk 1 stock at Nottingham Victoria in about 1960. The view is from over the parapet wall of the ramp to the small yard on the south east corner of the station site. This was a favourite vantage point for photographers and train spotters, affording a fine view of the south of the station.

E Shelton

The front of the building was clad in limestone, relieved by red brick panels at first floor level, and structural support was provided by a steel frame. The main block of street level buildings on Milton Street measured 250 feet in width, 100 feet of which was taken up by a steel framed, glazed awning to shelter arriving carriages.

Elegant stone mullioned windows were incorporated into the design of the frontage, which was topped off by a series of richly ornamented Flemish styled gables. Inside the 104 foot Booking Hall, two luggage lifts connected to a white glazed brick subway that crossed beneath the entire site, connecting with the platforms. The Booking Office was timber panelled, and the floor was laid in oak parquet blocks.

A graceful six storey 170 room hotel was built in red brick to the south of the station in a similar architectural style to the main station block, with covered access connecting it to the station. A folding ramp down to a carriage dock was constructed on the north side of the station, with access through a pair of wrought iron gates which bore the initials of the GCR and the GNR.

Above : 1950's advert for the Victoria Station Hotel from the Author's Collection.

The station's signalling was controlled by four cabins. Victoria North and South were large boxes located in the cuttings at the extremities of the site. These were busy places indeed, and required several personnel to operate them. The East and West cabins were built into the blocks of buildings on the island platforms, as projecting bays. These controlled minor shunting movements, and were never intensively used. Train register entries for South and East boxes are reproduced in Appendix 1.

Above: Colwick B1 No 61299 of Langwith Junction waits In Platform 10 with an excursion train in 1959. Parcels stock occupies the east dock in the background. *C A Hill*

Below : O1 No 63867 of Annesley Shed is seen passing the east turntable with a southbound goods on 16th February 1955. ***N(B)MRS*** */ D R Morley*

Above : Austerity No 90428 of Colwick Shed (40E) is seen in the centre road at Nottingham Victoria in 1965. The elegant glazed facing to the train shed was removed at the outbreak of the Second World War and replaced with ugly corrugated sheeting, spoiling the appearance of A E Lambert's design and blocking out much of the light inside.

C A Hill

6.2 Victoria at Work

Victoria Station was substantially engineered, with generous provision for trains and passengers. Arguably it made too generous a provision. Traffic never really grew to the degree that investors had hoped for, and the railway had arrived at a time when the market for new lines was slowing down. On normal weekdays, the station seldom appeared really busy, and local suburban services faced stiff competition from the Nottingham Corporation's new electric trams, which commenced operation in 1901.

Even if major growth traffic had materialised, it is questionable whether the station could have handled a seriously intensive main line service. The two track tunnels north and south were bottlenecks to operation, and the lack of separate freight lines would have led to conflicting demand between passenger and freight workings for limited train paths.

Appendix 1 contains extracts from Victoria South Box Train Registers, which reveal something of how busy a place the station must have been.

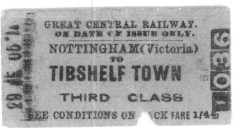

Nottingham Victoria was briefly named "Nottingham Joint Station", before its formal naming in 1901. It was jointly operated by the GNR and the GCR. The top ticket was issued by the GN, prior to its renaming, whilst the lower one shows the Station's more familiar name, and was issued by the GCR on June 25th 1905.

Ian Askew Collection

Left : ROD No 63645 of Staveley Shed (39B) passes Victoria North cabin with a southbound freight on 16th Feb 1955. An unidentified K3 is being turned in the background. The original GCR name board on the cabin was replaced with a maroon enamelled one after the London Extension transferred to the LMR in 1958.

N(B)MRS / D R Morley

Smartly timed expresses connected the north with the capital, as the builders had intended, and "The Master Cutler" became the line's best known passenger service. The South Yorkshire Pullman also offered speed and comfort, but smart timings were not limited to express passenger services.

The London Extension was predominantly twin-track, with few loops. This meant that freight services had to run at passenger train timings if they were not to delay the passenger services. A variety of freight traffic used the line, including fish from Grimsby and steel from Sheffield. Perhaps the best known freight movements were the Annesley to Woodford coal trains. Known in later years as "Runners" or "Windcutters", these were loose coupled, unfitted workings of tremendous length, a feat made possible by the gentle curves of the line and the generous yard facilities at each end. Robinson 04s, and in latter years BR Standard 9Fs ran these trains right up to the line's 75mph speed limit. There was a 10mph speed limit through Victoria, but even so, the noise echoing off the cutting walls as these workings passed through was impressive. This noise was added to by the report of gongs placed just inside the tunnel arrival roads. These treadle operated devices were triggered by arriving trains, the noise being intended to warn personnel in the vicinity of the presence of trains.

A southbound "Windcutter" is checked by the signals by Parliament Street bridge. The rear of Boots new store can be seen in this view. This building replaced the little used south pedestrian entrance to the station.

E Shelton

An unidentified Class C12 is seen making a somewhat smoky departure from platform 9 with a train for Derby Friargate, composed of ex GNR articulated stock, some time after the Grouping.

Author's Collection

Class O1 No 63857 is seen emerging from Mansfield Road Tunnel with a southbound freight in this 1958 view. The tunnel bore lacked smoke vents and was perpetually smoke filled.

C A Hill

SPECIAL NOTICE

ON and FROM

MONDAY, 20th FEBRUARY, 1956

A REGULAR PASSENGER TRAIN SERVICE

WILL OPERATE ON

WEEKDAYS

between

SUTTON IN ASHFIELD TOWN

and

NOTTINGHAM VICTORIA

as below :—

	SX	SO	WSO	SX	SX	SO	SX
	am	am	am	am	pm	pm	pm	pm
Sutton in Ashfield Town dep.	7.19	8.10	8.35	10.24	12.19	1.54	2.12	6.26
Hucknall Central ...... ,,	7.32	8.23	8.48	10.37	12.32	2.7	2.25	6.39
Nottingham Victoria .. arr.	7.45	8.36	9.1	10.50	12.45	2.20	2.38	6.52

	WSO	SX		SX	
	am	am	am	pm	pm	pm
Nottingham Victoria .. dep. 6.25	7.15	9.25	11.25	1.15	5.44	10.25
Hucknall Central ...... ,, 6.37	7.27	9.37	11.37	1.27	5.56	10.37
Sutton in Ashfield Town arr. 6.52	7.42	9.52	11.52	1.42	6.11	10.52

WSO—Wednesdays and Saturdays only.
SO—Saturdays only.   SX—Saturdays excepted.

NO SERVICE ON SUNDAYS

SPECIAL CHEAP DAY TICKETS

ANY TRAIN — ANY DAY

(on day of issue only)
between

Sutton in Ashfield and Nottingham	Hucknall Central and Nottingham	Sutton in Ashfield and Hucknall Central
2/1	**1/3**	**1/6**

(PLEASE CUT OUT AND RETAIN FOR REFERENCE)

BRITISH RAILWAYS

Thompson B1 No 60156 of Colwick Shed faces south in the centre road with a local passenger train on Wednesday 16th February 1955.

N(B)MRS / D R Morley

An unidentified Ivatt Class 4 departs Nottingham Victoria tender first, with a train for Derby Friargate in 1960.

C A Hill

Local passenger services ran out of the bay platforms at each end of Victoria, but this was not always straightforward. Trains for Basford and Bulwell via Daybrook would depart south, whilst trains for Basford & Bulwell, and on to Derby Friargate would depart north, thanks to a quirk of local railway geography. In the line's final years there was even less predictability, with southbound trains departing from the north bays then reversing direction.

There were other equally important services aside from passenger workings or heavy freight haulage however, and the night mail service was one of these.

During the 1920s the Author's grandfather was employed by the Nottingham Guardian, with its offices located a short distance from the station. One of his jobs was to meet the mail train in the early hours of the morning, and to collect their consignment of national papers for the coming day. He was given a three wheeled delivery bicycle for this task, but the basket on the front was too small, so a second bike would be towed on a length of rope. There were few people around at that time of the morning, so upon arrival at "Vic", both bicycles would be sent careering down the footbridge steps to the platform below, saving the trouble of getting somebody to operate the lifts. Once the train had arrived and the papers safely collected, the loaded bicycles would then be returned to road level by the more official and less exciting means of the luggage lift.

The relatively late construction of the line meant that its facilities were comparatively modern. Passengers were well catered for, goods and parcels facilities more than generous, and signalling was fully track circuited to provide safer train operation. Consequently there was little change or investment needed during its sixty eight year operational life.

6.3 The End of an Era

The story of the decline of Nottingham Victoria is a microcosm of the decline of railways nationally. Over provision by optimistic Victorian builders resulted in costly infrastructure without traffic growth to pay for it. Profitable freight revenues provided a degree of subsidy, but as the Twentieth Century progressed, competition from trams and then motor traffic took away patronage. Two World Wars, government intervention and restructuring of the companies, first into the "big four", then into British Railways, failed to reverse the decline.

In 1958 the London Extension became part of British Railway's London Midland Region. This region also controlled the Midland's Erewash Valley line and the lines out of Midland Station. The new regional management team set about finding ways of cutting costs, and consolidating operation. The rationalisation programme saw a transfer of many services from the GC route to the Midland route, which may have brought about an overall saving, but burdened the GCR with a disproportionate operating deficit. Consequently, Dr Beeching's 1963 report on the reshaping of Britain's railways recommended closure of the GC route.

Ivatt J6 No 64202 of Colwick Shed gets a clear signal for departure from Platform 8. The train, comprising Gresley suburban stock is bound for Derby, and this scene, recorded in 1958 had changed little in thirty years or more.

C A Hill

The shape of things to come: English Electric Type 4 No D209 is seen in Platform 7 with the Up York-Bournemouth at Victoria in the winter of 1958. Colwick J6 No 64257 waits in platform 12 alongside with a local train.

C A Hill

Five years after the previous shot, and DMUs have displaced steam on many workings. Station signs are now the corporate maroon of the LMR, and remaining steam workings are handled by LMS designs such as Stanier Class 5 No 44984.

E Shelton

The final years of steam operation saw an absence of LNER or GC types. Here an Ivatt Class 4 occupies the centre road, with a rake of ex LMS stock. An unidentified Standard Class 5 stands in the east bay and fitted vans occupy the west bay.

E Shelton

Trains to London finished in September 1966, when the line closed to the south of Rugby. Local services clung on for another year, but in September 1967 Victoria closed its doors forever. The remaining passenger service to Rugby was transferred to the hastily reopened Arkwright Street Station, until this was abandoned in 1969.

After the closure of Nottingham Victoria, iron ore trains destined for Stanton Ironworks continued to pass through the station site as it was progressively demolished. These too finished however in May 1968 and the last tracks were lifted.

Freight lingered on to the south for a while using a singled track from London Road via Weekday Cross Junction. Gypsum traffic served Hotchley Hill, and Ruddington MOD Depot saw movements of stores and vehicles. This finished in 1974 and the last main line was finally laid to rest.

When this Rugby bound DMU was photographed in 1961 the decline of the station was all too apparent. The line serving Platform 11 has been lifted. The introduction of Multiple Unit working meant that the bay loop was no longer needed for running around, and the downturn in traffic meant that both platform faces of the bay were no longer needed.

C A Hill

Above : Blue brick retaining walls dwarf Contractor's plant engaged in site clearance. Years of neglect have led to a tremendous amount of vegetation growing out of the brickwork.

Below : Remnants of Victoria North Signal Box still litter the ground three decades after it was demolished. The enamelled lamp once hung from the soffit board of the roof on the south end. The cabins in the background stand in the area once occupied by the carriage dock.

Left: The north cutting and Mansfield Road Tunnel portal lay abandoned for thirty years, before the Victoria Centre was extended to the north. The site has been cleared in this view, and the reinforced concrete skeleton of the new multi storey car park is beginning to take shape.

6.4 Nottingham Victoria : Surviving Fragments

Victoria station was quickly demolished, to be replaced by a shopping centre, bus station and multi-storey car park. Two freight lines remained in situ until May 1968, when the final freights on this portion of the GCR were diverted away. When the Victoria Centre opened in 1971, the only visible clues to the former station's existence were the clock tower and the north cutting with Mansfield Road tunnel entrance.

The clock tower was refurbished in the 1980s, and a significant part of the facing brickwork was replaced. Regrettably the new bricks were a different size and colour to the originals, compromising the towers appearance and its originality.

Beneath the feet of busy shoppers on Parliament Street lies the steel bridge built by the Great Central. Now hidden from sight, the bridge incorporated a four foot high tunnel for services. This is still used, and is seen here in 2005 during an engineering inspection.

The north cutting found no immediate reuse, and over a 30 year span developed its own distinct ecology, with rare plants and wildlife thriving in the heart of the city. At one point in the 1970s local radio announced that the site was to be used for a nuclear fall-out shelter. This proved to be an April Fools Day joke, but the site was eventually redeveloped in 1997. Slow worms and orchids were relocated before the multi-storey car park was extended north. A small portion of the cutting space has been left together with access to Mansfield Road tunnel portal, safeguarded for possible light rail use.

The Author took part in an engineering inspection of the tunnel in 2002, and an account appears in Appendix 5.

Less apparent remains of the station, hidden lie beneath the feet of busy shoppers. The glazed brick-lined 14 foot wide parcel tunnel that crossed the station still exists deep in the bowels of the shopping centre, today carrying service pipes. The substantial steel bridge carrying Parliament Street over the railway is also still in place. The intact structure, complete with smoke baffles is, only visible from inside the multi storey car park. It is from here that the outlines of the massive retaining walls and Union Road bridge abutments can also be discerned. The underground car park extends south into the cutting beyond Parliament Street Bridge, and finishes at a concrete block wall with a small door in it.

Thurland Street Tunnel is seen in 2005. The interface between cut and cover construction and tunnel heading is marked by a step in the tunnel roof construction. Steam of a different kind continues to use the tunnel, The pipes carry steam from the District Heat Station on London Road into the Victoria Centre to heat the flats and shopping arcade. The photograph was taken during a general inspection in 2005. The cleanliness of the brickwork is notable. In steam days it is unlikely that clean mortar joints would have been visible.

Beyond the locked door is a void extending the full height of the old cutting, dominated by the old tunnel portal and its curved wing-walls. The tunnel has been used to route pipes for the District Heat system, but the site of the Down Line is clear, and the original ballast still in place. A few sleepers, oddments of rusting signalling equipment and other items of railway interest are still scattered along the length of the tunnel, which was blocked at the south end in 2006 by construction of Nottingham's Contemporary Arts Centre.

A ghostly reminder of the London Extension, deep in the gloom of Mansfield Road Tunnel in January 2002. Two sleepers complete with chairs remain in place from the Up line.

Physical remains are it seems not the only reminders of the station to have survived. Many Victoria Centre staff are acquainted with supernatural activity, particularly in the lower levels at the south end of the site. Several ghosts have been repeatedly seen, and sightings have been corroborated by independent witnesses. One apparition of a middle aged man wearing a jacket and flat cap frequently appears, and has been seen by the Author's wife on more than one occasion over the five years she worked there. Research has suggested a connection between this figure and a fatal accident at the station just before it opened in 1899.

Victoria Station continues to fascinate, long after its demise. Numerous books have been written about it, surviving memorabilia now commands enormous

prices, and the City Council even briefly considered recreating elements of the stations ground level approaches in front of the clock tower.

One ambitious project was undertaken by friend of the Author and long time Local Councillor John Tanner, who recreated a substantial portion of the station in miniature. This splendid OO scale model featuring the booking hall and clock tower has appeared at several model railway exhibitions in Nottingham, and has featured in a number of local papers. It even appeared at the launch of the Three Centuries of Transport website, an archive created by Leicestershire County Council and several partner organisations that includes the photographs of S W Newton, who recorded the construction of the Great Central in 1898.

Just how long the fascination with Victoria Station will last remains to be seen. Interest in the long departed behemoth seems not just limited to those that remember it. The Author has been involved with a number of events connected with the GCR, and some of those people showing greatest interest in John Tanner's model could not have been born until well after the original was demolished.

Nottingham Victoria recreated in miniature. The model of the booking hall is almost four feet wide, and the clock tower stands nearly two feet high.

6.5 Towards Basford and Points North

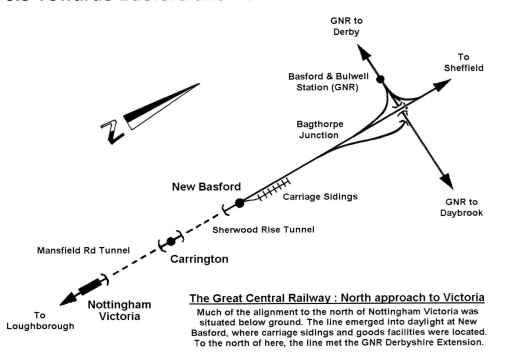

To Loughborough — Nottingham Victoria — Mansfield Rd Tunnel — Carrington — Sherwood Rise Tunnel — New Basford — Carriage Sidings — Bagthorpe Junction — Basford & Bulwell Station (GNR) — GNR to Derby — To Sheffield — GNR to Daybrook

The Great Central Railway : North approach to Victoria

Much of the alignment to the north of Nottingham Victoria was situated below ground. The line emerged into daylight at New Basford, where carriage sidings and goods facilities were located. To the north of here, the line met the GNR Derbyshire Extension.

To the north of Victoria, the line burrowed through sandstone for 1189 yards on a rising grade of 1 in 132, before briefly emerging from Mansfield Road Tunnel into daylight at Carrington. Here a small station with facing platforms served this prosperous and gentile outskirt of the city. Situated in a deep cutting, the station buildings were some distance away, at road level, and connected by a long ramp. The two platforms were joined by a lattice steel footbridge, and shelters were provided at platform level. An intermediate block post signal cabin stood on the Up platform at its south end.

Third Class ticket of the type issued for journeys to and from Carrington Station in LNER days. This example was issued at Bulwell Hall.

Ian Askew Collection

Carrington Station had been closed for thirty years, when this unidentified Austerity locomotive was recorded working a northbound engineer's train on 27th April 1963.

Ronald Askew

Twenty years later and the trains had gone. Although the tracks and anything of salvage value had gone, there were still significant remains to be seen, including platforms, tunnel portals, a signal post and the abutments to the footbridge.

Beyond Carrington Station, the line again burrowed deep beneath the Bunter Sandstone, climbing through Sherwood Rise Tunnel at 1 in 130 to emerge 662 yards on, in the deep rock cutting that marked the approach to New Basford Station. This station was built to the standard island configuration, with access from steps through the abutment of the adjacent road bridge. The station itself was fairly modest, but it had a substantial goods yard and a 100 foot long two storey goods shed. To the north of the station, on the up side were carriage sheds and servicing facilities, including a plant for manufacture of gas for coach lighting.

Above : "Black 5" No 44717 draws out of New Basford Goods Yard with a mixed rake of stock early in 1962. Sherwood Rise Tunnel is partially obscured by smoke in the background, which was a frequent occurrence in the days of steam traction.

C A Hill

Top Right : Thompson L1 No 67769 runs into New Basford from the south with a local passenger service destined for Derby Friargate during the winter of 1958. The outer distant for Carrington has a back board to aid sighting because of its low mounting position.

C A Hill

Bottom Right : K3 No 61842 of Colwick Shed restarts a Derby train from New Basford in snowy conditions in 1960. The lattice steel parapet of Haydn Road over bridge was boarded in as a protective measure for the public highway beneath. Access to New Basford Station was up steps that ran through the south abutment, roughly beneath where the engine is situated.

C A Hill

Top Left : Britannia Pacific No 70036 Robin Hood of Immingham Shed is seen approaching New Basford at speed with an Up fish train during the summer of 1963.

Neill Fisher

Bottom Left : Valley Road bridge was built by the LNER in 1932 to carry the London Extension across the new Nottingham Ring Road. The original GCR pattern Bagthorpe Junction signaL box stood here, and was replaced with an LNER design box a little further to the north. The bridge is seen in 1980, just before demolition.

Nottingham City Council

Below : Bagthorpe Junction marked the northern limit of joint ownership of the London Extension. Here connections to the GNR's Derbyshire Extension joined on Up and Down sides. Austerity No 90554 is seen heading south with a Colwick bound mineral working in 1962.

C A Hill

Travelling north from New Basford, the line drove through one last ridge of sandstone to pass beneath Perry Road, this time in a deep rock cutting, before emerging onto a tall embankment and crossing Valley Road, as it approached Bagthorpe Junction and the first of two connections with the GNR Derbyshire Extension.

Bagthorpe Junction marked the northern limit of the GN/GC joint ownership of the route and the GN was crossed over close to Arnold Lane. The second junction at Bulwell South was met a short distance after this, and the line pushed north up the Leen Valley towards Annesley and beyond.

To the north of Bagthorpe Junction, the line crossed Arnold Lane. This short section of road was crossed by four lines in total, two passing over and two beneath. 9F 92132 of Annesley Shed is seen heading north with a "Windcutter" in 1962. The parapets of the bridge across the GNR Up connection can be seen in the foreground.

C A Hill

6.3 South to the River

To the south of Victoria, the line again disappeared below ground, following the line of Thurland Street in a shallow cut-and-cover tunnel, which gave way to a heading at the south end of Thurland Street. The line emerged from this midway up a steep escarpment at Narrow Marsh, and the GNR branch to London Road High Level Station, and to Grantham peeled sharply away to the east at Weekday Cross. This marked the southerly extent of joint ownership with the GNR.

The London Extension strode confidently south across Canal Street, the Nottingham Canal and the Midland Railway, and on through the Meadows on a 1000 yard long series of viaducts and steel spans, heading for the River Trent and beyond. A station perched atop the viaduct where the line crossed over Arkwright Street, which was at that time the main road south out of the City to Trent Bridge.

Arkwright Street Station buildings were, from an architectural point of view, a strange jumble of oddments. They were crammed into a small space between the

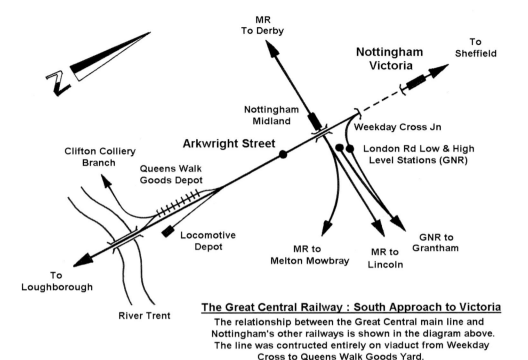

The Great Central Railway : South Approach to Victoria

The relationship between the Great Central main line and Nottingham's other railways is shown in the diagram above. The line was contructed entirely on viaduct from Weekday Cross to Queens Walk Goods Yard.

two steel bridge spans of Waterway Street and Arkwright Street, and the existing properties that the GCR had left in situ. Much of it was crammed into the arch space within the masonry abutment, and the remainder was built for functionality rather than appearance. Unusually for the London Extension, the station had two platforms flanking the running lines.

Above : A third Class ticket issued on 3rd June 1901 for a journey from Arkwright Street Station to Bulwell Common. This particular example was printed on green card and is typical of GCR tickets of this period.

Ian Askew Collection

The old Guildhall was demolished at Weekday Cross to make way for the railway. The south tunnel portal is seen here in 1979, five years after the last tracks had gone. After the lines were lifted, Thurland Street Tunnel was reused for the City's new District Heat System.

Stairs and lifts from ground level were situated in a pair of towers at the north end, and the ticket office, and other facilities were located off these where space permitted. There was no overall architectural style to the buildings, and the ground level entrance was a domestic looking affair attached to earlier terraced properties. In addition to those plans shown in this chapter, several of the original architect's drawings for Arkwright Street Station and approach bridges are reproduced in Appendix 6.

The platforms at Arkwright Street were carried trestles supported by steel piers alongside the masonry structure that supported the lines. They were bounded at the back with a close boarded 6' timber fence. Simple awnings provided shelter for passengers, but otherwise minimal facilities were located at platform level.

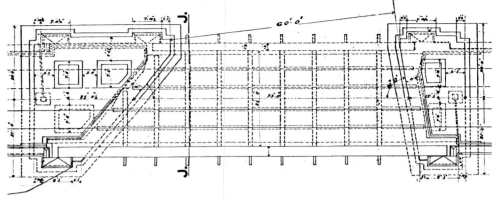

Plan Courtesy Nottingham City Council

A bowstring girder bridge spanned across Canal Street. This was trapezoidal in plan, with the east elevation (seen below) being considerably shorter than the west. The deck was suspended beneath, which maximised headroom for road traffic. Today a replacement structure catties trams across Canal Street at this location.

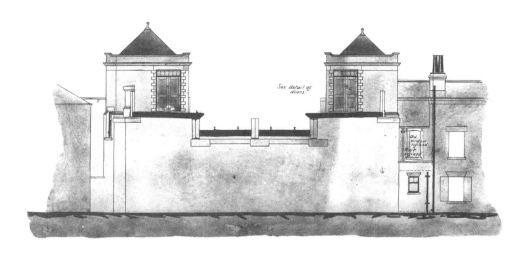

— Section D.D. —

The section above is looking north, and cuts through the wide masonry abutment that sat between Arkwright Street and Crocus Street bridges. The existing terraced properties to each side of the railway structure were retained, and the new station buildings constructed right up to them.

Ian Trivett Collection

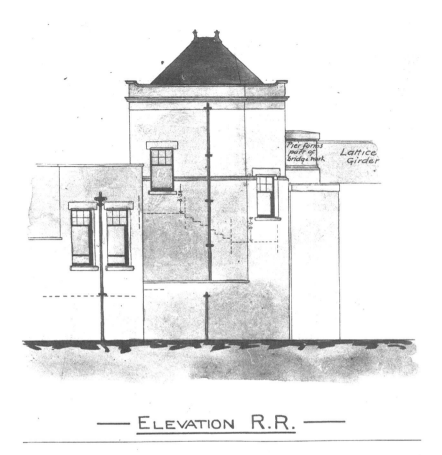

— Elevation R.R. —

The stairs from street level to the platforms were housed in a pair of towers at the north end of Arkwright Street Station. This 1897 colour washed architect's drawing shows part of one of the towers, with windows at each landing on the stairway.

Ian Trivett Collection

To the south of Arkwright Street Station the GCR built a 33 acre goods yard, a motive power depot and a carriage shed. The goods warehouse measured 150 feet in length and had two floors. It was equipped with three loading platforms and wagon turntables to each end. In addition to various hydraulic and electric hoists and capstans, a 25 Ton Goliath electric crane was provided for heavy loads. At the southern end of the goods yard, a branch led away to the nearby Clifton Colliery, which had until that point solely been served by the Midland Railway.

The Engine Shed had four roads, with sufficient depth to accommodate four engines in each. A fifty foot turntable was provided for the turning of engines.

Separate freight lines paralleled the main running lines through the goods yards, and south across the River Trent bridge, providing a goods loop for a half mile length.

The crossing of the Trent (Bridge No 289) was one of the larger structures on the line. Of over 800 feet in length, it comprised three trussed girder spans of approximately 130 feet each, with extensive flood arches to each side. The length of each flood arch made it necessary to construct archways between them, through each pier. This feature allowed hydrostatic pressures to equalise in times of flood. A separate plate girder through-deck bridge (Bridge No 288) crossed the Victoria Embankment. All of the bridge spans and flood arches were doubled up, in order to carry the additional goods lines, which resulted in a very substantial structure. The form of design for the trussed girders and the slender suspended deck resulted from the Trent Navigation Company's requirement that sufficient headroom be maintained for commercial river traffic.

Immediately south of the river, the four tracks merged back into two, the junction and southern yard entry being controlled by a fifty five lever signal box (Nottingham Goods South) positioned between the central pair of tracks. After withdrawal of services south of Rugby, the yards and freight loops were removed, and in 1967 the box was abolished and stripped.

Bridge 288 was a plate girder design with very deep webs to allow for the 66 foot span needed to clear the Victoria Embankment. It was demolished in 1985.

Nottingham City Council

6.7 Reclamation

Whilst Victoria Station disappeared within months of its closure, the abandoned routes feeding into it lingered on for years and even decades afterwards.

The first appreciable section of route to be reclaimed was ironically the last section to see trains, and stretched south to the River Trent. In 1974 before the last gypsum working had even departed from Hotchley Hill, Nottingham City Council was drawing up plans for the removal of the Great Central across the south of the City. A multi-million pound redevelopment of the Meadows area was programmed to clear several square miles of Victorian terraces and to remove the old grid-iron pattern of streets. The GCR traversed this area, and the City was under pressure to maximise its delivery of modern inner-city low cost housing. Consequently the viaduct south of Queens Road was demolished in 1975/6, and the area it occupied together with Queens Walk Goods Depot was swiftly replaced with high density urban housing. Only the Goods Depot offices were to survive, and are in City Council ownership at the time of writing.

The Trent crossing succumbs to the attentions of demolition contractors in 1985. Temporary trestle supports allowed the main trussed girders to be cut into pieces and lifted out. The stripped deck was then cut into sections and removed. Today there is no trace of this structure remaining.

Bridge 289 is seen here in the early 1980s. The bracket signal controlling exit from the Up goods loop can just be discerned to the south of the river.

The largest steel structure on the Nottingham section of the line, the quadruple track, three-span crossing of the River Trent lasted a little longer. In 1982 it was temporarily used to carry a diverted pedestrian route to Wilford village whilst the adjacent Wilford Bridge was closed for reconstruction. After this was completed in 1984, the redundant structure was dismantled and its approach viaducts demolished.

The bridges over Midland Station, Queens Road and Station Street were removed in 1978, to be followed by Canal Street over bridge in 1980. The remaining steel bridges at Cliff Road and Garners Hill were dismantled in the late eighties, leaving the masonry elements of the viaduct in situ from Station Street to Weekday Cross.

The final remains of the structure seemed to be granted a reprieve when they were earmarked for use as part of a proposed light rail development. Although this scheme eventually came to fruition, the bulk of the structure was not reused. The arches between Canal Street and Cliff Road were demolished in 2001. Five arches between Station Street and Canal Street, including the skew arch across the Nottingham Canal were used, and have a long term future assured.

The scale of the 1980 reclamation project, and the amount of land that it freed up for development can be gauged from this photograph of the approach to Bagthorpe Junction, taken from Valley Road in September of that year. The GNR burrowing spur ran behind the excavator and the embankment carried the main line, together with the western GN spur. This area is now occupied by housing.

Nottingham City Council

In 2003 the viaduct that carried the lines from Weekday Cross to Canal Street was demolished to make way for a new bridge, to carry NET (Nottingham Express Transit).

To the north of Victoria, the GC and GN joint route lay abandoned and surprisingly intact for a decade and a half. Indeed as late as 1980 cast iron signs still warned against trespass on the railway at several locations near Bulwell, and lines of telegraph poles and stumps of signals still flanked the empty track bed as it stretched away to the north.

Above : Hucknall Lane over bridge was one of three bridges removed during 1981. Preliminary clearance works are underway in this photograph taken by the City Council's Site Engineer.

Nottingham City Council

In August 1980, the City Council embarked on the first phase of a major land reclamation scheme. This would eventually remove all structures and earthworks associated with the GC and its connecting lines, from Perry Road at Sherwood, right through to Bulwell. A substantial area of land would be released for development, and the local authority would be relieved of its maintenance liability for a redundant asset.

Structures to be demolished over the next 18 months included the LNER's 1932 steel plate girder bridge, across the Ring Road, the lattice steel three span footbridge at Paton Road, and the northern section of Bulwell Viaduct including the steel span over Hucknall Lane. Other bridges to be infilled included St Albans Road, Bulwell Common access, Perry Road and the GN bridges beneath Arnold Road.

First the vast embankment at Bagthorpe junction was progressively excavated with the spoil hauled along the railway alignment to areas of cutting. Here it was deposited and compacted in layers, until gradually all cutting areas were filled. Next the over bridges were demolished.

On a cold January day in 1982, Paton Road footbridge is lifted off its piers on to a waiting low loader in readiness for reuse over the River Leen at Basford.

Nottingham City Council

Tragically during the demolition of Valley Road Bridge, a Senior Engineer from the City Council was killed after falling through an unguarded excavation in the deck of the bridge above Valley Road.

Following an investigation the work resumed. The deck of the bridge was craned off its abutments and cut up on adjacent land, whilst the red brick abutments were demolished with machine mounted hydraulic breakers. Paton Road footbridge deck was also craned off its piers, but a section of the span was taken away for refurbishment at a local engineering firm. This was subsequently reused to carry a footpath across the River Leen at Basford, at the same site where the GNR Derbyshire Extension once crossed the river.

The infilled cuttings were left to consolidate for two years before new housing development began to spring up, but construction on the former embankment sites began immediately. By the mid-1980s most of the reclaimed land was used, and few traces of the railway remained.

Carrington Station was in a sorry state by 1987. The Booking Hall is visible at the top of the picture and in use as a Newsagents shop. The track bed was becoming overgrown, and the platform edges and sites of the demolished buildings were becoming difficult to see. The copings above the tunnel had also been pushed off.

Two interesting parts of the formation to escape the land reclamation scheme were the sites of Carrington and New Basford stations. Carrington was located in a short cutting between Mansfield Road and Sherwood Rise tunnels. After the track recovery train left in 1968, much remained. The platforms, minus edges were left in situ, together with redundant concrete signal posts, footbridge abutments and rubble from the demolished signal box. The portal to Sherwood Rise Tunnel was bricked up, but Mansfield Road Tunnel remained open, beckoning the brave, or foolhardy to walk through to the Victoria Station site. The street level booking office also remained, converted into a tobacconist. The end came in 1987, when the site was sold for development. The cutting was infilled, the Booking Office demolished, and a sheltered housing complex built above the station site.

New Basford probably retained more of an atmosphere of a working railway after closure than any other GC location in Nottingham. When the Author visited the site in 1983, the coal depot and goods yard were still busy, with original offices, staithes, weighbridge all in use. The generously proportioned goods shed remained occupied and in good order, and although the station buildings had gone, the Station House survived in private ownership, in good condition.

The tracked was surprisingly clear right up to Sherwood Rise Tunnel, which was set in an impressive sandstone cutting. Retaining walls marked the location of the demolished signal box, and stumps of signals were still visible in places. It was also possible to discern the level and edge of the station platform on land that had been incorporated into a neighbouring factory yard.

Sadly the goods shed suffered fire damage in 1984 and the site was cleared for redevelopment shortly after. The final traces of New Basford Station were

removed In 2006, when a housing development was built on neighbouring industrial land, and the southern abutment, together with its blocked off stairway that once led to the platform was demolished.

The cutting leading to Sherwood Rise tunnel was filled with imported spoil in the 1980s, and a new access road was built into the site. A housing development now occupies much of the area. One fragment to remain is the retaining wall, built to accommodate the signal box and lampman's hut, but which now retains the gardens to several new houses.

In 1989 the last portion of Bulwell Viaduct was demolished to make way for a retail development, and complete the removal of the line in the north of the City.

The railway that was to be the last main line, and which dramatically reshaped Nottingham at the end of the Nineteenth Century has now all but vanished. Today few clues remain above ground level to show that the GCR ever existed in Nottingham.

New Basford Goods Shed is seen here in around 1985, as demolition is starting to commence. The roof has been removed and the end is not far. The main line ran to the right of the picture and the area of raised ground in the middle distance by the silo was once the island platform. Today this are is occupied by a housing estate, with nothing to show that a railway ever existed

Neill Fisher

Beyond the housing estate that occupies the site of New Basford goods yard is a playground and recreation area, created on the site of the filled in cutting. To the south of this, the cutting is not completely filled. A scramble through the bushes is rewarded with the discovery of the upper portion of Sherwood Rise Tunnel. This was blocked off at both ends and used as underground storage for many years, before the cuttings at each end were filled. The tunnel itself was not infilled, and remains hidden from view.

7. High Level Station and the GC Connection

New Alliances, New Routes

The arrival of the GCR's London Extension in 1899 was to change the face of railway geography in Nottingham. The GNR had realised early on that access to the new centrally located station would offer significant advantages in its rivalry with the Midland. The company was on amicable terms with the GCR, having co-operated on joint ventures elsewhere in the county. An agreement was struck that it should contribute, and share in the ownership of the new line from its intersection with the GN Derbyshire Extension in the north, through the centre of the city, to a junction with a new GN link at Weekday Cross.

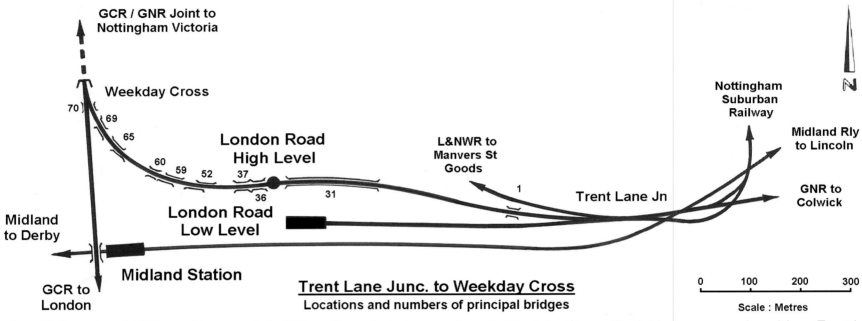

Trent Lane Junc. to Weekday Cross
Locations and numbers of principal bridges

The Great Northern Railway Act of 1895 sought powers to build from the projected main line at Weekday Cross, over Canal Street and across the Nottingham Canal, to link with the existing GNR line. The point of connection would be to the north side of the Company's London Road terminus, at the western end of the No 1 Departure Platform. Presumably the Company thought better of running the new services through the busy goods yard area and over a level crossing on London Road, because the route was amended under a further Act in 1899 with a more northerly route starting at the junction complex to the east at Trent Lane.

Under the revised arrangement, a new elevated station would be provided to face the existing one, and the tracks would cross above London Road. The revised alignment was to be elevated for its entire length, and space constraints meant that virtually all of it was carried by structures, rather than embankment. This very expensive stretch of line required 70 spans to cover the mile or so from Meadow Lane to Weekday Cross. The bridges were numbered from Trent Lane Junction, and each span, including individual arches, was given a unique number and fitted with a cast iron bridge plate.

In April 1904 a Third Class single from High Level to Hougham, on the East Coast Main Line, near Newark would have cost you just under two shillings. Today neither station exists.

Ian Askew Collection

Trent Lane Junction is seen looking west along the truncated Suburban Railway Up line in 1957. The tracks to the far right lead to Manvers Street Goods Depot, with a 20T brake just visible in the mist. The next pair pass between the telegraph poles towards High Level and Victoria, whilst the remaining tracks lead to London Road Low Level Station.

C A Hill

Bridge No 1 crossed Meadow Lane in a single 35ft skew span. It comprised 3 main steel girders, with trough decking and lattice parapets. It was demolished in December 1993, and the site its west abutment is now the entry to Gresley Close. This official photograph is from the District Engineer's bridge records and dates from about 1903. Note the ghostly images of children on the right, caused by the slow shutter speed of the camera.

Author's Collection

Ten spans were steel bridges, and they included two substantial crossings of the Nottingham Canal (Bridge Nos 36 & 52) and a lengthy steel trestle across sidings to the north of the Nottingham gasworks (Bridge 31). The remaining 60 spans were blue brick faced arches, many of which were subsequently bricked in and rented out as workshop space.

The new intermediate passenger station was built facing the old GN terminus. Its setting was less than picturesque, being hemmed between the canal and Boots Works to the north and the Nottingham Corporation's gasworks to the south. The new station was named London Road High Level and to avoid confusion, the old terminus was renamed London Road Low Level. A string of modest timber buildings were provided along the central island platform of the new station, flanked by glazed canopies supported on cast iron columns. A single storey red brick booking office was provided at ground level, facing south. Passengers entered through double doors into a booking hall finished in beige glazed brick, relieved with two narrow horizontal bands of dark brown.

The windows of the booking office were on the left, and a white glazed brick archway led to the trains, with a 30 cwt lift for luggage, and three flights of stairs to platform level on the right. When the station was first built, a small signal box perched on the side of the viaduct to the west of the booking hall. This was abolished in 1930, with the whole line becoming a single block section from Trent Lane to Weekday Cross.

To the east of the passenger entrance the station was supported by four masonry arches (Spans 32 to 35), the external faces of which were bricked up, with windows incorporated into the curtain walling. These arches had interconnecting tunnels, and access to these was taken from the store rooms to the side of the booking hall, and also through the abutment of Bridge 31. The portion of arch beneath the platform was constructed with greater headroom and a reduced arch thickness to reflect the lighter loading above. These areas beneath the station were used for stores and workshops, with internal entrance ramps to allow trolleys and sack trucks to negotiate the level difference.

The first section of viaduct was split into two discrete sections of arches, the second of which is seen here alongside Sneinton Hermitage in 1987. This element comprised arches 15 to 30.

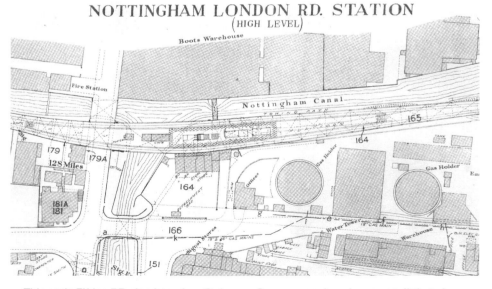

NOTTINGHAM LONDON RD. STATION
(HIGH LEVEL)

This early Fifties BR plan based on Ordnance Survey mapping shows very little to have changed around High Level since its opening in 1899. The Nottingham Canal still ran alongside the Boots factories and Town Gas was still in production to the south of the railway. The individual spans of each arch and steel bridge are shown in a pecked line.

High Level Station was well used and prosperous. The Boots Pure Drug Company had numerous manufacturing sites in the immediate vicinity, and the station was well placed to serve its large workforce. Workers from the many textile companies nearby also benefited from local services. The station was close to Notts County's Meadow Lane ground, and within walking distance of Nottingham Forest's City Ground, making it a busy place when teams played at home. Cricket fans also used the station, being invited to "alight for Trent Bridge" on the stations running-in board.

Arch 30 and Bridge 31 are recorded here in another official view, looking west. The steel structure comprised 19 individual spans, each nominally 49 feet long. The curious cross girder arrangement at the end of each span allowed the gasworks sidings to pass beneath the bridge and access the canal wharf beyond. Part of the gasworks can be seen beyond the wall. The reason for the pile of wicker baskets in the foreground is something of a mystery.

Author's Collection

The British Railways era

Passing into BR Eastern Region ownership in 1948, nationalisation had little immediate effect and for the next decade the line and its station continued to be busy. Restructuring of BR's regional boundaries in 1958 brought the station under Midland Region control and with it a change of fortune. The line was now part of a duplicate network, and services were progressively pruned away. In 1960 trains heading for the 'Back line' finished, and in 1964 all services for Grantham were diverted into Nottingham Midland. In September 1966, connecting long distance services finished at Victoria.

In spite of the reduced service, passenger receipts continued to be high. The stations fortunes were inextricably linked however with those of Victoria. The impending closure of the Great Central inevitably meant the end of High Level. In June 1967 the station closed its doors to passengers for the last time, despite account sheets showing that the station was still turning a profit.

After closure, the platform buildings were demolished and the street level buildings mothballed. Stanton Ironworks trains continued to use the line, but with the lifting of freight lines through Victoria in May 1968, this working finished. That was not quite the end however. A short section of the GC remained open to serve the Gypsum works at Hotchley Hill near Rushcliffe Halt, and the Army's Ordnance Depot at Ruddington. No convenient access existed to the south, so the line remained open north to Weekday Cross Junction, and a single connecting line was left in place through High Level. Freight trains reversed inside the tunnel at Weekday Cross and again at Trent Lane to regain the main line.

The western end of Bridge 31 is seen here. The Down Starter for High Level Station is "off" indicating the approach of a train. This structure was demolished in around 1979 to make way for warehousing. The abutment in the foreground survived until 2006, when it and the warehouse were cleared for new development.

Author's Collection

Gypsum and military stores continued to be shuffled across the Nottingham viaducts until 1974, when a connection was built between the Midland main line and the GC to the north of Loughborough, allowing a more practical access arrangement.

High Level Station found a new use after closure. The building was leased to two separate firms, one supplying office furniture and the other shipping antiques. In 1982 it was vacated, and the buildings were sold for use as a railway themed restaurant.

After the Trains

Rails were lifted and the alignment was finally abandoned in 1974. Demolition of the GN line began in 1978 when a section of viaduct and the Bridge 37 over London Road were removed to facilitate road improvements. Canal Street bridge (No 59) followed shortly after, together with the steel viaduct (Bridge 31) to the east of High Level Station.

The latter structure has been quoted as having a reputation amongst some enginemen for its elastic behaviour under load. However flexible it may have been, the structure survived in service without need of any major repairs for eighty years, in a sulphurous and corrosive environment sandwiched between a chemical plant and a gasworks. Indeed most of the original structures were still in place largely untouched at closure. The exception was the short steel span of Bridge 70 crossing Cliff Road.

Bridges 36 and 37 are recorded here in January 1978. Bridge 37 over London Road is shortly to be removed and a crane is already in position. The generous headroom available above the Nottingham Canal allowed Bridge 36 to be built using trussed girders. This bridge would be removed 19 years later in 1997. The platform of High Level Station extended across both bridges and as far as the third arch on the left (span 40). The Boots Island Street premises are seen in the background. Today these and the railway are just memories.

In the Sixties the edge beam and parapets were renewed. The bridge originally had plate steel parapets like the adjacent GCR structure, but why they were changed so late in life is a mystery. The deck was removed in 1982.

Bridge 36, carrying the western end of the High Level station across the Nottingham Canal proved more difficult to lift. In 1996 Nottingham City Council employed Contractors to demolish the twin steel trusses. The largest mobile crane in Europe was brought in to lift the spans out. With London Road closed, and watched by local television news cameras and hundreds of spectators the lift began. The first truss had barely moved when warning bells sounded in the crane's cab and the lift had to be promptly aborted. The weight of the truss appeared to be greater than first supposed. The road was reopened, and embarrassed Engineers began their investigations.

The structure's reprieve was to be short lived. Two weeks later a second attempt was made, and both spans were successfully lifted onto the site of the recently demolished Boots Island Street Works for cutting up.

The remaining steel bridges were also removed during the Nineties, with the last to go being the second canal crossing (bridge 52) in 1999. The canal side brick arches succumbed in the same year to an urban regeneration scheme.

From Span 51 to 46 the brick built south parapet gave way to a steel handrail. This may have been a later modification to the original structure, and certainly the large pipes seen here were. They carried steam for the District Heating System from London Road Heat Station

Time finally ran out for the arches beneath High Level station and the booking hall building in 2006, when they too were demolished. These had survived for many years as an antique dealer's warehouse, before being redeveloped as an American Style 'Diner'. It went through several incarnations, and at one stage it had even been mooted to reinstate tracks and place "dining coaches" alongside the platforms above. This never took place but an industrial saddle tank stood outside for some years, lending to the "railway theme". The property latterly became part of the "Hooters" chain, and was demolished in March 2006.

The site of the line will eventually become a mixed use development, with businesses, and apartments, and where gasworks once stood, a landscaped lake.

At the time of writing, the only remaining infrastructure is a short section of viaduct to the west of Popham Street (spans 66-68). These are destined to be demolished in 2007 to make way for a new bus station, and once they have gone, no trace of the route will remain.

Bridge 52 crossed the Nottingham Canal on a skew angle of more than 45 degrees. with the skew span measuring over 96 feet, as against 45 feet on the square. Despite abandonment of the railway, this view remained little changed for a century, before removal of the bridge in 1999. This official view is believed to date from 1903 and comes from the District Engineer's bridge records.

Authors Collection

The Nottingham Canal ran right alongside the viaduct for a considerable distance, and the towpath was surprisingly narrow. This view from 1998 shows between spans 40 and 50. To the south side lay Boots Print Works

Bridge 59 is recorded here by the Great Northern's Official Photographer in around 1903. The width of Canal Street is little changed today, although the same cannot be said for the volume of traffic! The mass of advertising posters on the hoarding include such familiar brands as Bovril, Vim and McDougall's Flour. The design of the bridge is similar to No 53 over the Canal. The Bridge Engineer's record card states that the square span was 60 feet, and the skew span 86 feet 10 inches. The steel trusses were supported on roller bearings and the deck floor comprised of steel plate. Completed in 1899, this structure was demolished by Nottingham City Council in 1980.

Author's Collection

Bridge 59 is seen again in 1979. The Great Central's bowstring girder bridge that carried the London Extension can be seen in the distance. Both bridges were demolished by the City Council during 1980.

Bridge 60 was the smallest steel bridge on the line, with a square span of just 13 feet. The bridge number is visible on the right hand abutment. In 1903 is appears that a house could be let for the princely sum of three shillings and eightpence (presumably for the week). Some of the housing stock in this part of Broad Marsh was particularly bad, and much had been cleared by the Thirties. Bridge 60 was removed in about 1982.

Author's Collection

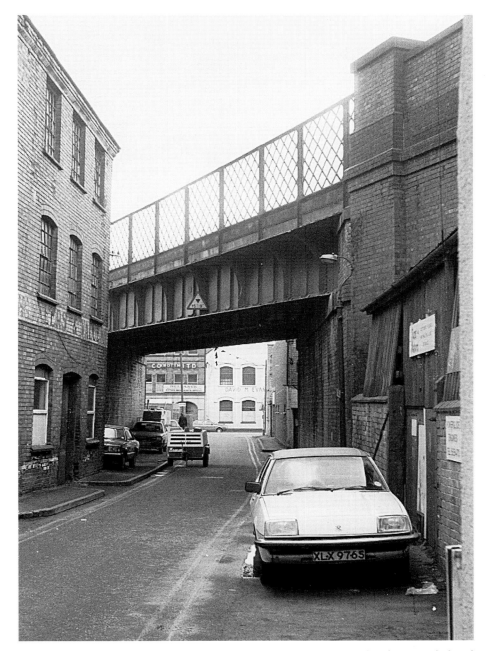

Bridge 64 over Popham Street was difficult to photograph owing to the close proximity of industrial buildings and its skew angle. The design of this structure was similar to Bridges 37 and 70, but with three main beams supporting the plate steel deck. It is seen here in 1982, just prior to demolition.

This desolate scene was recorded in about 1980. It shows Bridge 69 across Malt Mill Lane, and the brick base of Weekday Cross signal box standing in the apex of the junction with the Great Central's viaduct.

Bridge 70 crossed Malt Mill Lane almost immediately beneath Weekday Cross Junction. The edge beam and parapet were renewed very late in the life of the line. The BR standard type open steel design replaced a plate steel parapet of GCR design.

Nottingham City Council

Weekday Cross junction finally lost its tracks in 1974, five years before this view. The pipes and structure on the trackbed are part of the Nottingham District Heating Scheme that was built in the early Seventies.

The reverse view to the above shows the tunnel portal at Weekday Cross, with the alignment of the Joint Line stretching towards Victoria. By the time of this March 2006 view, Victoria had long gone and the area pictured was about to be built on.

End of the Line

The following views record the removal of the route over twenty five years. Much of the reclamation work was carried out by the City and County Councils, with the Author being personally involved in a couple of these schemes.

Above and top right: The steel trusses of bridge 36 were lifted off and cut up in November 1996 as part of the City Council's reclamation of the old Boots Island Site. The crane used to lift the truss was the largest of its kind in Europe. The upper halves of the roller bearings are clearly visible in both views.

Bottom: The same Down Line truss is seen here some months earlier, before the deck had been stripped. The large span that necessitated the deep truss can be appreciated in this view. Barges like the one moored in the foreground were used to transport much of the demolition rubble from the Boots factory on Island Street.

In the early Eighties the High Level station building was refurbished and extended. A fifth bay was added to the eastern end of the structure in a matching style, and the brickwork was blast cleaned to reveal much detail that had been lost beneath layers of white paint, applied during its spell as an antiques shipping warehouse. Unfortunately the new owners did not favour natural brickwork, and the masonry was painted over shortly after this picture was taken.

The view below shows the curving sweep of the platform face on the Down side of the station

Above : Although the platform buildings were removed in the late Sixties, their outlines were clearly visible in the form of quarry tile floors, rotting oak parquet blocks and most surprisingly the white glazed urinal bases where the Gents lavatories once stood. The octagonal base of a cast iron canopy support is visible in this view looking east.

Below: One of the original GNR bridge plates still in situ in on the north face of the structure in March 2006. Many of these plates were still in place when the structures were demolished.

Removal of the much altered Booking Hall building during demolition revealed the original glazed brick finish that the interior of the buildings and subway had originally been finished in. The Beige and contrasting brown bricks were supplied by Farnley Ironworks Limited of Leeds, whilst the white bricks of the arch lining came from the Leeds Fire Clay Company .

The bricked up entrance through the abutment is visible in this view taken during final demolition in April 2006. The higher profile of the central portion of the arch which supported the platform can clearly be seen.

The area beneath arches 32 to 35 had been used for storage during the stations time as a restaurant. During railway service it had been used as workshops and stores. A ramp led through the abutment of Bridge 31 to the yard outside, enabling hand trolleys to negotiate the level difference.

Cast iron column bases and sections of reinforcing bullhead rail lie in the rubble, together with the cast iron strip drains from the floor of the Gents urinal. The base of each column had a 4 inch cast pipe protruding from it, suggesting that rainwater from the canopy was channelled inside of each column, eliminating the need for downpipes.

In late 1993 Contractors cleared the Sneinton railway lands to facilitate redevelopment of the area. A large slice of the masonry viaduct carrying the High Level line had been demolished 18 months before to allow construction of a new road linking Manvers Street with Daleside Road. This second set of works removed completely every last trace of the line from its approach to Bridge 1 over Meadow Lane, up to Arch 32 beneath High Level Station itself. This selection of views records the demolition in progress.

The Bridges between Weekday Cross and London Road were removed progressively between 1980 and 2007. In the case of each contract, tracked plant had to be craned onto the old trackbed to remove the parapets and copings. The main masonry sections were demolished with hydraulic excavators and breakers, and the steelwork was lifted out by crane. Today nothing remains of this line or its engineering works

Appendix 1

Selected Train Register Entries
Nottingham Victoria South Signal Box

BRITISH RAILWAYS _____ South Signal Box **DOWN LINE** 18th Dec 19__ 35 B.R. 24665

Train Registers can make dry reading, but they do occasionally provide glimpses into the more interesting aspects of day to day railway operation. An example is recorded above, where a Down freight was stopped at Victoria North for examination, because the Duty Signalman at Victoria South thought the first wagon behind the locomotive was running with a flat on a wheel. The examination found nothing, and the train was allowed to proceed, but the incident illustrates the sort of matters requiring a Signalman's attention, in addition to the main business of operating block instruments, pulling levers and checking that the clock is correct.

An entry from the next page of the same 1959 Register records another problem with a freight movement, this time with sparks flying from a vehicle indicating a possible brake fault. The entry was made at 12.40am, when the sparks would have been easy to spot in the winter darkness.

DOWN — Nottingham Victoria South Signal Box — Satur day, 27 day of June 1964 — B.R. 24847/1

The above extract is from a 1964 Train Register for Victoria South Box. By this date traffic was in decline and top link express locomotives were virtually a thing of the past. Saturday 27th June seems to have been an exception however. At 16.51, Peppercorn Pacific No 60125 'Scottish Union' arrived with a Down passenger train. It was unusual to see an LNER designed Pacific on the Great Central at any stage, let alone by this late date, and it was sufficiently noteworthy to be recorded in the Train Register (see bottom line). Ex GWR Halls were more familiar to the route, but by 1964 were also something of a rarity, hence No 6911 'Holker Hall' also merited a special note against the 16.24 arrival.

Trawling the depths of such documents reveals something of the routine encountered by a Signalman at a large box some 40 or 50 years ago. In the few areas where traditional signalling survives today, these typical Train Register entries will have a familiar ring to the present generation of Signallers.

Appendix 2

Whistle Signals for Shunting Movements at Colwick
(From LNER Appendices to Regulations May 1942)

Colwick—
Rectory Junction Box

Derby line Up Main and Derby line Up Slow	5 short
Derby line Up Main and Derby line Down Slow	2 short
Sidings 1 or 2 to Up Main	1 long, 1 crow
Up Slow to Engine Spur	1 crow
Down Main to and Up Main from Nottingham	1 long
Down Main to Avoiding line	1 crow
Down Main to Arrival lines	3 short
Down Main to Down Slow	5 short
Down Main to Derby	2 short
Up Avoiding line and Up Main	1 crow

Colwick—

Box	Movement	Whistles
Rectory Junction Box	Engine Spur to No. 1 Arrival	1 short
	Engine Spur to No. 2 Arrival	2 short
	Engine Spur to No. 3 Arrival	3 short
	Engine Spur to No. 4 Arrival	2 short, pause, 2 short
	Engine Spur to No. 5 Arrival	2 short, pause, 3 short
	Engine Spur to No. 6 Arrival	3 short, pause, 3 short
East Junction Box	Avoiding line Inner Home to Down Main	5 short
	Avoiding line Outer Home	2 short
	Avoiding line Up Advance	2 short
	Down Main to Up Avoiding line	2 short, pause, 2 short
	Exchange Sidings to Down Main	3 short
South (Pointsmen) Cabin	Nos. 1, 2 and 3 Arrivals to Engine Road	3 short
	Nos. 1, 2 and 3 Arrivals to West Group Sidings	3 short, pause, 1 short
	Nos. 1, 2 and 3 Arrivals to East Group Sidings	3 short, pause, 2 short
	Nos. 4, 5 and 6 Arrivals to Engine Road	6 short
	Nos. 4, 5 and 6 Arrivals to West Group Sidings	6 short, pause, 1 short
	Nos. 4, 5 and 6 Arrivals to East Group Sidings	6 short, pause, 2 short
	Up Avoiding line and Arrival lines	3 short
Carlton Field Box	West Group Siding and Up Main	1 long, 1 crow
	Western Group Sidings and Up Slow	2 long, 2 crow
	Western Group Sidings and No. 1 Shunt line	5 short
	L.M.S. Group and No. 2 Shunt line	6 short
	L.M.S. Group and Departure Road	According to destination
	Departure Road and Up Slow	2 long, 2 crows
	Departure Road and Up Main	1 long, 2 crows
	Eastern Group 12 to 21 and No. 3 Shunt line	3 short
	Eastern Group 12 to 21 and Up Slow	2 long, 3 crows
	Eastern Group 12 to 21 and Up Main	1 long, 3 crows
	Eastern Group 22 and 29 and No. 4 Shunt line	4 short
	Eastern Group 22 and 29 and No. 3 Shunt line	3 short, pause, 3 short
	Eastern Group 22 and 29 and Up Slow	2 long, 4 crows
	Eastern Group 22 and 29 and Up Main	1 long, 4 crows
	Down Slow	2 short
	Down Slow and Arrival	2 short, 1 crow
	Down Slow and Up Main	1 crow, 1 short
	Down Main and Arrival	1 short, 1 crow
	Goods Yard and Arrival	3 short, 1 crow
	Goods Yard and Down Slow	3 short
	Engine line and Up Main	1 long
	Engine line and Goods Yard	1 long, 3 short
	Up Slow to Sidings, set back	3 short
Locomotive Junction Box	Departure line to Engine line	2 short, pause, 2 short
	Engine line to Spur	2 short
	Loco' or Spur to East Junction	4 short
	Loco' or Spur to L.M.S. Loco'	2 crows
	Up Engine line Stop	5 short
	Down Engine line Stop	5 short
	Cripple and Lay-by Sidings to Loco'	1 crow, 2 short
	Cripple and Lay-by Sidings to Yard	1 crow, 1 long
	Directing Signal to Loco'	5 short
	Directing Signal to Engine Spur	2 short
	Directing Signal to Departure Road	2 short, pause, 2 short
	Down Engine line to Down Slow	5 short, pause, 2 short
	Engine Road to Engine Shed	5 short
	Engine Road to Engine Spur	2 short
	L.M.S. Loco' to Engine Shed	2 crows
	L.M.S. Loco' and Engine Shed	1 crow
	Engine Spur to Up Engine line	1 long
	Engine Spur and Eastern Empty Sidings	4 short
	Engine Spur and Western Empty Sidings	3 short
	Sidings 1 or 2 to Engine Spur	1 long, 2 crows
	Old to New Yard	3 short, pause, 3 short
	Eastern Sidings and Shunting Road	4 short, pause, 4 short
	Eastern Sidings and Yard Road	4 short, pause, 3 short
	Eastern Sidings and Down Slow	4 short, pause, 2 short
	Eastern Sidings and Down Main	4 short, pause, 1 short
	Western Sidings and Shunting Road	3 short, pause, 4 short
	Western Sidings and Yard Road	3 short, pause, 3 short

Colwick—*continued.*

Box	Movement	Whistles
	Western Sidings and Down Slow	3 short, pause, 2 short
	Western Sidings and Down Main	3 short, pause, 1 short
	Down Engine line to Spur	1 long
	Engine line to Spur	1 crow
	Entrance to L.M.S. Loco'	2 crows
	Down Main to Up Engine line	1 short, pause, 1 long
	Down Main to Sidings	1 short, pause, 3 short
	Down Slow	2 short
	Down Slow to Main	5 short
	Down Slow to Up Engine line	2 short, pause, 1 long
	Down Slow to Sidings	2 short, pause, 3 short
	Up Yard to Yard Road and Engine line	3 crows
	Up Main and Eastern Reception Sidings	4 short
	Up Main and Western Reception Sidings	3 short
	Up Main to Nottingham	2 short
	Down Siding No. 2 and Down Grantham line	2 short
	Down Slow and Down Grantham line	5 short
	Up Siding No. 1 and Down Grantham line	1 short, 1 crow
	Up Siding No. 1 and Up Spur	1 crow, 5 short
	Western Group of Reception Sidings and Down Main	2 short, pause, 3 short
	Western Group of Reception Sidings and Up Spur	1 crow, 3 short
	Eastern Group of Reception Sidings and Down Main	2 crows, 4 short
	Eastern Group of Reception Sidings and Up Spur	1 crow
	Eastern Engine line and Up Spur	6 short
	Up Spur and Up Grantham line	1 crow
	Up Spur and Up Nottingham line	1 crow, 2 short
	Down Main and Up Grantham line	4 short
	Down Main and Up Nottingham line	2 short, pause, 2 short
	Down Nottingham line and Loco' Siding	1 long, 2 short
	Down Grantham line and Siding	1 long, 1 short
	Loco' Siding and Spur	1 crow
	Engine line and Grantham Up Main	1 crow
North Jct. Box	Engine line and Loco' Yard	1 crow, pause, 1 crow
	Up Spur and No. 1 Reception Siding Western Group	1 short
	Up Spur and No. 2 Reception Siding Western Group	2 short
	Up Spur and No. 3 Reception Siding Western Group	3 short
	Up Spur and No. 4 Reception Siding Western Group	4 short
	Up Spur and No. 5 Reception Siding Western Group	5 short
	Up Spur and No. 6 Reception Siding Western Group	6 short
	Up Spur and No. 7 Reception Siding Eastern Group	1 crow, 1 short
	Up Spur and No. 8 Reception Siding Eastern Group	1 crow, 2 short
	Up Spur and No. 9 Reception Siding Eastern Group	1 crow, 3 short
	Up Spur and No. 10 Reception Siding Eastern Group	1 crow, 4 short
	Up Spur and No. 11 Reception Siding Eastern Group	1 crow, 5 short
	Up Spur and No. 12 Reception Siding Eastern Group	1 crow, 6 short
	Up Spur and Engine line	2 crows, 5 short
	Engine line and Dead End	3 short, pause, 3 short
	Engine line and Down Grantham Main	1 short, 1 crow
	Loco' Yard and Dead End	1 crow
	Loco' Yard and Down Grantham Main	1 long, 1 short
	Loco' Yard and Up Spur	1 crow, pause, 1 crow
	Dead End and Engine line	3 short, pause, 3 short
	Dead End and Grantham Up Main	4 short, 1 crow
	Dead End and Nottingham Up Main	1 long, 2 short
	Loco' Outlet and Dead End	3 short
	Loco' Outlet and Grantham Down Main	1 long, 2 short
	Loco' Outlet and Up Spur	3 short, 1 crow
	Nottingham Down Main and Engineer's Siding	2 short, 1 crow

Gedling—

Box	Movement	Whistles
Colliery Box	Up Main and Run-round Road	1 long, 1 short
	Up Main and Full Sidings	1 long, 2 short
	Colliery line and Up Main	3 short
	Run-round Road and Spur	1 crow
	Full Sidings and Spur	2 crows
	Down Main and Colliery	2 short
	Up trains and Light Engines on approaching East end of Miner's Platform	1 long
	Down Freight trains requiring water at Daybrook, **on passing**	1 crow

Appendix 3

Special Instruction for working the Nottingham Suburban Railway (From LNER Appendices to Regulations, May 1942)

NOTTINGHAM SUBURBAN LINE.

Drivers of trains working through from Daybrook to Nottingham must take the train staff forward to Nottingham Goods Yard Box and from there it must be taken by the London Road Passenger Station staff and sent to Daybrook by Passenger train. The staff must be handed to the Station Master at Daybrook and he must see that it is placed in the Daybrook Signal Box in readiness for the Freight train the following morning.

Freight trains from the direction of Daybrook requiring to work at Sherwood will stop on a sharp rising gradient and the special attention of Guards is drawn to the necessity for securing their trains in accordance with the instructions in Rule 115 (c) before uncoupling the engine.

The Signalman at Trent Lane must be advised by telephone when the train is ready for leaving Thorneywood.

Appendix 4

Nottingham Suburban Railway : Demolition Mishap

Nottingham Guardian report from 1954 on accident during removal of bridge No 1. Fortunately there were no injuries during the mishap, but today such an incident would have serious repercussions, with the HSE being notified, and a HMRI investigation.

TRAINS HALTED BY FALLEN GIRDER

Railway traffic between Nottingham and Lincoln was restricted to single-line working yesterday following an accident at Trent-lane.

At this point the Victoria-Thorneywood - Daybrook suburban line crosses the line to Lincoln, and the bridge, made dangerous by war-time damage, is being demolished. During early morning work, a girder, which was being hoisted by a 40-ton crane, slipped and fell. Nobody was hurt, but the track was obstructed for about seven hours.

An emergency bus service was operated between Carlton station and Nottingham until single-line working was restored.

1954 report about accident during removal of bridge (Nottingham Guardian)

Appendix 5

Mansfield Road Tunnel
Engineering Inspection

On 11th January 2002 I accompanied Engineers from Nottingham City Council's Structures Office, on a general inspection of the abandoned Mansfield Road tunnel to the north of what had once been Victoria Station.

The Highway Authority have an interest in the stability of the structure since it runs directly beneath Huntingdon Street and Mansfield Road. This was the first official inspection in over a decade and the first formal entry since the northern portal was filled over in the late 1980's.

On the day of the inspection, the weather was clear and cold. Negotiating the small hole in the hoarding across the south portal we entered the tunnel, and faced a wall of mild and very still humid air. A peculiar mist rose from two feet above the floor and extended to the roof. Our flashlights struggled to penetrate it. Stepping carefully, we edged our way into the gloom. About ten metres into the tunnel, the blue brick wall lining ended. The abutments from here comprised soot encrusted sandstone. On the side of the Up line, timber brackets projected from the rock. The remains of cables that were once supported by these lay on the ballast with the sheathing stripped away.

A wooden cable trough ran along the back of the Down line cess; many sections of this were broken and displaced. Tucked against the Down side of the tunnel, a broken gradient post still indicated a rising grade towards Carrington Station, although the numbers had long gone. Close to the entrance the remnants of a timber signal post that once controlled Up trains leaving the tunnel were still buried in the abutment. Nearby a few pulleys and odd parts of point mechanism littered the trackbed, together with rusting beer tins, old council road lamps, bicycle frames and the inevitable shopping trolley.

After the first 50 metres or so, the mist disappeared and our lamps were better able to pierce the deep gloom, revealing the tunnels curve to the left as it headed north. Quickly we lost sight of the portal, and what little natural light there was. Keeping no more than 20 paces apart to keep visual contact with each other, we pushed on. Refuges with arched blue brick lintels were cut into the rock at frequent intervals on each side, once providing safe haven for men working on the permanent way. Capped with blue brick, these seemed to be well preserved.

Concrete pillars projected from the Up line cess. Permanent way gangs used these as reference points, to set the cant on the rails. A variety of railway related debris was strewn along the ballast, and the further we went, the more we saw. Broken accumulators, fishbolts, wooden bullhead keys and an insulating bullhead rail joint insert were readily identifiable, along with anonymous pieces of what may once have been point rodding. Curiously amongst these oddments were parts of a wagons vacuum brake gear. Any ferrous material was extremely corroded.

From 200 metres the tunnel began to curve to the right. This must have limited forward visibility for drivers and made sighting of signals difficult. The corroded remains of colour light signal fixings andl ladders were still in place, and several sleepers complete with chairs represented the last fragments of the Up line.

At 500 metres, on the Down side we found a much larger recess in the abutment. Inside were the broken remains of a red oxide painted wooden cabinet containing smashed accumulators. This would have provided power to the S & T equipment (presumably track circuits) via cables in the wooden troughs in the cess. A similar alcove on the Up side contained a rusting filing cabinet, the remains of a steel framed chair and an old bed frame.

Proceeding onwards, accumulator cases continued to litter the trackbed, together with more wooden keys. The remaining section of tunnel was much the same as the rest. Approaching the northern portal the amount of rubbish increased, and the amount of abandoned railway equipment fell off. The portal itself was blocked off with an in-situ concrete wall, right on the entrance. A ladder led to the base of an inspection chamber, which led to the surface.

The final hundred metres of the tunnel were fully brick lined, and water dripped from the soffit onto the miscellaneous construction debris and rubbish that littered the trackbed. A broken concrete gradient post lay in the Down cess just inside the portal, together with several point rodding rollers.

The walk back felt to be much quicker than the walk up, although the down grade helped.

Summary

From inspection it was apparent that the blue brick roof to the tunnel was in good condition, with no major defects or leaks. The tunnel seemed remarkably dry which explained why discarded timber fittings showed few signs of decay. In fact the tunnel was exactly as left when the tracks were lifted in 1968.

The sandstone abutments were showing minor signs of deterioration. The rock was friable in places along the seating of the blue brick roof lining, and a small drift of sand lay against each abutment. This had probably been accumulating over a long time period and may relate to moisture content in the naturally soft exposed rock. It does not represent an immediate problem, but the tunnel will continue to be monitored.

There are no immediate plans for Mansfield Road Tunnel. A feasibility study proposed its use for the NET project some years ago, but given the difficulty in regaining access to the north end, there is little likelihood of trams ever using it. In all probability it will remain mothballed indefinitely, a hidden relic of Nottingham's railway past.

Appendix 6

Arkwright Street Station Engineering Drawings

(From the collection of Ian Trivett)

Street level entrance to Arkwright Street Station, adjacent to bridge abutment.

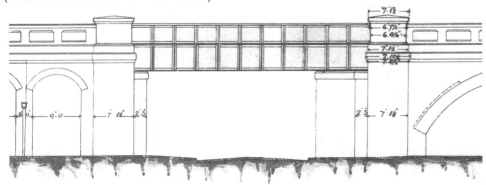

Elevation of Crocus Street overbridge from original GCR drawings

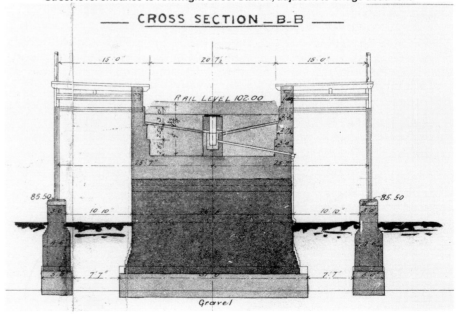

CROSS SECTION — B-B

RAIL LEVEL 102.00

Section through structure supporting platforms

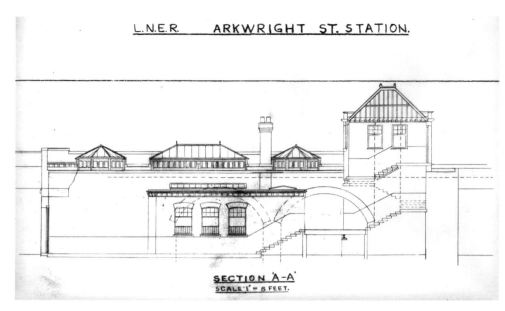

L.N.E.R.   ARKWRIGHT ST. STATION.

SECTION 'A-A'
SCALE 1" = 8 FEET.

Elevation of station buildings prepared during LNER days for renewal of station lighting

Bibliography

Whilst numerous information sources were used during the research of this book, specific reference was made to the following publications and documents. Every effort has been made to ensure that information is reproduced correctly, however any errors or omissions are wholly the Author's responsibility.

Institution of Civil Engineers
Paper No 3227 20th March 1900
The Great Central Railway : Northern Division
F W Bidder

Great Northern Railway Act 1880
Indicative Alignment Plans
(Reproduced from Ordnance Survey Mapping)

The Great Northern Railway
O S Nock

The Midland Railway
C Hamilton-Ellis

History of the Midland Counties Railway
C T Goode

The Great Northern Railway in the East Midlands Vols 1-4
A Henshaw

The Midland Railway around Nottinghamshire Vol 1
G Hurst

Passengers No More
G Daniels & L Dench

An Illustrated History of Great Northern Railway Signalling
M A Vanns

The Development of Nottingham's Railways
J P Wilson

The Railways of Newark on Trent
M A Vanns

Signalling Atlas & Signal Box Directory of Great Britain & Ireland
P Kay

The Great Central Then & Now
M Hawkins

Ordnance Survey County Series 1:2500 mapping.

Acknowledgements

The Author is indebted to the following individuals, organisations and companies for their assistance during the writing of this book. Their contributions, through allowing access to private collections and unpublished reference material, and arranging permission to visit restricted sites has considerably elevated the status of the completed work and broadened the Author's knowledge along the way.

Ian Askew
Geoff Brain
John Bull
Tom Hawkins
Ian Trivett
John Mulhall
Building Design Partnership Ltd
BWB Consulting Ltd
Eastside & City
Greenhatch Surveys Ltd
Laing O'Rourke
Network Rail
Nottingham (Bulwell) MRS
Nottingham City Council